GOKHALE AND ECONOMIC REFORMS

GOKHALE AND ECONOMIC REFORMS

A Brief Account of
the Patient and Persistent Agitation for Economic Reforms
Carried on by the Late Hon'ble, Mr. G. K. Gokhale,
in the Viceroy's Legislative
Council and Outside

VAMAN GOVIND KALE, M. A.

GYAN

Published by

GYAN

Gyan Publishing House
5, Ansari Road
Daryaganj, New Delhi-110002
Phone: 011-47034999, 9811692060
E-mail: books@gyanbooks.com

Distribution Network
gyanbooks.com
India, USA, Canada, UK, Australia, France

ISBN: 978-81-212-8694-7 (PB)
First Published, 1916

2nd Impression 2023

Printed at: Gyan Press, Delhi.

GOKHALE AND ECONOMIC REFORMS
Author: Vaman Govind Kale

GOKHALE AND ECONOMIC REFORMS

A Brief Account of
the patient and persistent agitation for economic reforms carried on by the late Hon'ble Mr. G. K. Gokhale, in the Viceroy's Legislative Council and outside

BEING

A Thirty Years' Review of the Financial and Economic development of India.

BY

VAMAN GOVIND KALE, M. A.,
Prof. of History & Political Economy, Fergusson College, Poona.
Author of "Indian Industrial and Economical Problems" "Indian Administration" &c. &c.

POONA:
PRINTED AT THE ARYABHUSHAN PRESS.

1916.

PREFACE.

While reading Mr. Gokhale's speeches in the Viceroy's Council, I had been often struck with the persistence, the patience, the knowledge, the earnestness and the eloquence with which he urged, from year to year, upon the attention of Government, several financial and economic reforms calculated to promote the material and moral well-being of the people of India. I was also struck with the strong impression he could make upon the official mind and the manner in which he prevailed upon the Government to adopt some of his suggestions. It is not given to an Indian, however exalted his position and however great his talents may be, to shape the policy of Government except in a very indirect way and to an extremely limited extent. Mr. Gokhale's achievement, therefore, lay in having fought against odds and in the face of disappointment and in having attained a measure of success in his advocacy of the cause of economic reform which has not been equalled by any Indian leader. Owing to his repeated insistence upon the true principles of financial and economic reform and his sound, fearless and helpful criticism of the attitude and measures of Government, Mr. Gokhale's speeches have become peculiarly instructive to a student who wants to get an insight into this subject, and wishes to form his own views thereon.

It is on account of this feature of the speeches that I have always read them with profit and pleasure. A few days after Mr. Gokhale's death last year, I had occasion to contribute to a journal an article giving an estimate of his work as an advocate of economic reform, and later in the year, to read the speeches again along with other literature, in connection with my University lectures on Indian Finance. The idea then occurred to me of writing out a brief but connected account of the substantial contribution he has made to the discussion of various questions of economic importance and of presenting it to the public interested in the subject. I thought that such a summary would prove useful to the general reader as well as to the student-world, and this book is the realisation of that idea. I have tried to make plain, topics which are not free from technicalities and complexities and to treat them in a simple and popular way. How far I have succeeded in attaining my object, the reception the book meets at the hands of the public, alone can tell.

Mr. Gokhale is, of course, the central figure in this account, and his views constitute the main subject dealt with. But for a clear understanding of the topics discussed, a setting of the exposition of the principles underlying the various topics and of the general situation in which events occurred and measures were adopted, was felt to be necessary. I have supplied this in the proper places. Mr. Gokhale's advocacy of reforms was inspired with the uniform desire of seeking to promote the material and moral well-being of the people of India, and I have characterised them as 'economic,'-a word that is usually used in a narrowower sense. I have, of course, excluded from my purview his agitation for administrative and constitutional reforms, having only touched it here and there. The following pages thus trace the financial and economic development of India during the past 30 years, and will, it is hoped, make useful reading.

I am grateful to the Aryabhushan Press for the willing assistance they gave me in bringing out the book on the day of the first anniversary of Mr. Gokhale's death.

Fergusson College, Poona.
19th February, 1916.

V. G. KALE.

CONTENTS

Chapter I.

Pages.

UNDER TRAINING:—

Chapter II.

THE ORDEAL:—

Chapter III.

INITIATION:—

GOKHALE'S ECONOMIC REFORMS.

CHAPTER I.

UNDER TRAINING.

I. Gokhale's Unique Position.

Towards the latter part of his career, the late Hon'ble Mr. Gokhale occupied a unique position in the public life of his country. He enjoyed the confidence and the regard of his countrymen in a higher degree than any other Indian leader, except Mr. Dadabhai Naoroji, and his life of service and sacrifice won him universal admiration. He came to be regarded as the most faithful and reliable exponent of Indian feeling and opinion, both by Government and people, and his pure motives, his statesmanship and his patriotism were warmly recognized. Mr. Gokhale dominated the Supreme Legislative Council by his thorough grasp of the problems he handled and by his luminous, masterly and convincing manner of exposition. He was armed with facts and figures which he could marshal with consummate skill and perfect confidence. He was steeped to his finger-tips with the knowledge of the political and economic problems of India and could draw upon the rich store with ease. His knowledge had been completely assimilated, and Mr. Gokhale, by constant study and thought, had formulated definite principles of reform for which he fought with rare persistence and courage. His reading was wide and up-to-date, and the inspiration for reform had come to him through his study of the political and economic history of western countries and a constant pondering over the condition of his motherland. Intensely patriotic and national in his ideal, he had enriched his mind and widened his outlook by steady observation and thought. Though he died prematurely, he had devoted more than twenty five years of his life to the passionate study of Indian problems and his knowledge, experience, talents, eloquence and patriotism combined to place him in the foremost ranks of his countrymen and made him a towering personality in the Imperial Legislative Council. Such was the impression he had made upon that legislative body that Mr. Gokhale was sorely missed when he was, owing to illness, prevented for two years, in 1913 and 1914, from taking part in its debates. His absence was particularly felt at the time of the discussion of the financial statement and the Finance Member thought that without Mr. Gokhale the Viceroy's Council acted Hamlet with the part of the Prince of Denmark left out.*

---

* Closing the budget debate at a meeting of the Viceregal Council, on 24th March, 1913, Sir Guy Fleetwood Wilson remarked:—"It is difficult for those who served in previous Councils to express to those who are new to this Council what a great blank Mr. Gokhale's absence creates. It seems to be the play of Hamlet without Hamlet, and I think we all agree in wishing him a return to good health and a return to the Council next year."

Mr. Gokhale was looked upon as 'the leader of the Opposition' in the Supreme Legislative Council and performed the duties of that office with unprecedented success. But he never acted in the spirit of party and faction as leaders of opposition do in other countries. Popular representatives in our legislative bodies cannot, in fact, emulate the policy of the latter in as much as they cannot, under the existing Indian constitution, hope, by their opposition, to get into power which is permanently fixed in the hands of the officials. However strongly they may criticise the policy and measures of Government, they find it difficult to make an impression on the official attitude. Mr. Gokhale's criticism was invariably well-informed and delivered in the interest of reform and progress, and though the members of Government could not and would not openly admit its reasonableness and urgency, they had quietly to carry out some of the suggestions the people's leader threw out. When we review, in a later part of this book, Mr. Gokhale's agitation for economic reform, in the Supreme Legislative Council, we shall show how his labours were constructive and fruitful when he hammered away, year after year, at the problems of financial and material progress of India. It will be sufficient here to record the testimony of one of the officials who had often to bear the brunt of Mr. Gokhale's attacks on the policy of Government and who had to yield to their vigour, persistency and reasonableness. In 1912, Mr. Gokhale moved a resolution in the Viceroy's

Council urging the necessity of strengthening the financial position of Local Bodies and recommending the appointment of a committee for inquiring into the matter. In the course of his reply to his remarks, the Hon'ble Sir James Meston observed :—"Whenever Mr. Gokhale advocates a policy to which he attaches much importance, I am irresistably reminded of the Indian juggler who sows a mango seed in a flower pot and covers it over with a cloth. In an extraordinarily brief space of time he removes the cloth and behold there is a goodly mango tree in full bearing! So it is with Mr. Gokhale. He advocates a certain reform. We give him the mild answer which turneth away wrath, and we think we have before us an appreciable breathing time. But Mr. Gokhale has sown his little seed in his little flower pot; he has covered it over with his little cloth, and within an incredibly short space of time he removes his little cloth and presents to our astonished vision a tree bearing not only leaves, not only buds and flowers but a goodly crop of wholesome fruit."

In repudiation of the charge of incapacity and unfitness of Indians to fill responsible positions in the administration, Mr. Gokhale had once challenged the critics to try the experiment and confidently assured them that men like Ranade and Mehta would have creditably discharged the duties which great ministers in foreign countries performed. A similar remark might be made of Mr. Gokhale himself who, everybody said, would have made an ideal

Finance Member of the Government of India. Whatever truth there may be in the story that was at one time circulated that he was consulted as to his acceptance of the Finance Membership and that, for obvious reasons, he declined that offer, it shows the public estimate of his capacity. As critics of the policy and measures of Government, Indians are at a great disadvantage. They have no access to the sources of information which are open to European officials and non-officials, and they have no opportunities of getting first-hand knowledge of the machinery of administration. But Mr. Gokhale had overcome this difficulty by making himself thoroughly acquainted with the details of every question he took up and in this matter he could give points even to official members of the Legislative Council. When he was on his legs to speak, the officials were very uneasy as they knew Mr. Gokhale would hit the weak joints in their armour. He was never superficial, never ill-informed, never inaccurate and had no difficulty in demolishing the case made out by his opponents in favour of their measures or attitude. The story is told how, on one occasion, "Lord Kitchener privately asked him the points on which he wished to touch so far as military expenditure was concerned, and, out of consideration for the great soldier who was no debater, Gokhale did not emphasise certain points as much as he would have liked to." Such a predominance, in an assembly like the Supreme Legislative Council, which had not the backing of official prestige or authority, was the result solely of intellectual eminence, impressive eloquence, sustained and pains-taking study of public questions and a reputation for sincerity of purpose and purity of motive.

II. Ranade's Influence.

Very few of the people who admire Mr. Gokhale realise how in his early years he toiled and laboured for equipping himself for the life he had selected for himself. Endowed with a strong memory, he developed that faculty with the greatest assiduity, and the nervous English and the incisive eloquence of which he was a master, had been labouriously acquired. When he was called upon to teach classes in Fergusson College, he was entrusted, at the out-set with Mathematics, English, History and Political Economy. Though he taught all these subjects satisfactorily, he shone in the last two and they came to have a peculiar fascination for him. The public life of Maharashtra was at that time very stirring, and movements for all kinds of reform, social, political and industrial, were remarkably active. The late Mr. Justice Ranade was the soul of these movements, and his influence was all-pervading. He attracted and attached to himself all sorts of men, young and old, and inspired them with a desire to do some work for public good. Mr. Ranade exercised peculiar magnetic influence over all who surrounded him and imparted to them a touch of his own public spirit and enthusiasm in the cause of progress. He could detect with a singularly unerring eye the aptitudes of men and make them put forth their best, for the benefit of the country. Young, earnest and aspiring, Mr. Gokhale could not resist this force of attraction and was soon drawn into the orbit of Mr. Ranade's influence. And he proved himself an apt pupil of the great master from whom he picked up many of the qualities which characterised him in later life. His optimism, catholic sympathies, liberal tendencies, gentleness, urbanity, devotion to the study of public questions, breadth of vision, moderation and other traits of his character and career may be traced to this source. In the tribute he paid to his daparted *guru* at the memorial meeting held in Bombay in July 1901, Mr. Gokhale thus remarked:—' My friend, Sir Bhalchandra, has already referred to the extraordinary quickness with which Mr. Ranade discerned and encouraged all earnest workers in the country. He had a wonderful faculty in this respect and, as a result, he was, to many young men, scattered all over the country, like the central sun from whom they derived their light and warmth, and round whom they moved, each in his own orbit and at his own distance. The feeling of devotion that he was able to inspire in such men was most marvellous and to those young workers who were privileged to come in intimate personal contact with him, his word was law and his approbation their highest earthly reward. Mr. Ranade, in fact, possessed in the highest degree the ideal attributes of a great teacher".

CHAPTER I.

Even when he had himself become a great man, Mr. Gokhale often frankly and openly acknowledged his deep indebtedness to Rao Saheb, as Mr. Ranade was popularly called, and it is difficult to convey a correct idea of how much the pupil owed to his master. This contact of the two earnest and kindred souls began at a time when the Indian National Congress had just been started and filled the country with a new-born enthusiasm and when the condition and the political and economic problems of India were being discussed with peculiar zest in the press and on the platform. We have this fact from Mr. Gokhale himself who, addressing the Bombay Congress of 1904, on the question of surpluses with which the Indian Treasury overflowed during the *regime* of Lord Curzon, said :—"Gentlemen, it was more than sixteen years ago that I first imbibed a love for the study of financial questions at the feet of my great master, Mr. Ranade, and since then, I may claim to have been a fairly close student of Indian finance". It was thus about the year 1888-89 that Mr. Gokhale's apprenticeship commenced and his progress, as may be expected, was extraordinarily rapid. He was eager to learn, possessed the capacity to take infinite pains and had good opportunities for the exercise of his faculties. The *Sarvajanik Sabha* of Poona was then a very active public body, interesting itself in the well-being of the people and representing to Government, from time to time, their views, grievances and needs. Turning over the pages of the Quarterly Journal of the Sabha one is struck with the record of the active work the Sabha did, its memorials to Government, the correspondence it carried on with the officials on the questions of the day, and its discussion of the various administrative and legislative measures which affected the interests of the public. The Journal also published essays and papers on political and economic questions contributed by writers like Mr. Ranade and Rao Bahadur G. V. Joshi, which even at this distance, make instructive reading.* One sighs for the days when such public activities were possible in Poona. For about six years till 1896 when Mr. Gokhale severed his connection with the Sabha, he was the editor of the Journal and must have done a good deal of work in drafting the memorials of the Sabha and in other ways. He took part in public meetings and made speeches on the burning topics of the day on the Congress and other platforms. This was a period of Mr. Gokhale's apprenticeship to public life and he worked hard to make a way for himself to public leadership. Many of our aspiring young men forget that the path to eminence in public life is toilsome and rugged and that no one who wants to serve his country can do so without laborious training and painful experience. Mr. Ranade was uniformly courteous to everybody, but Mr. Gokhale was often made to feel when he read out to his *guru* or wrote

* These papers have been published among the collected writings of these two devoted students. Ranade's 'Essays on Indian Economics' contains several of his papers from the Quarterly Journal.

to his dictation that he was in the presence of a task-master. No true greatness is possible without preliminary training and discipline, and Mr. Gokhale had these in their due measure. We lay special stress on this point for the benefit of the rising generation, most members of which are anxious to shine and become great but unwilling to pay the price of that greatness. They applaud Mr. Gokhale's abilities and his knowledge, but scarcely realize that these were acquired by hard and incessant labour.

As we shall show in the later chapters of this book, Mr. Gokhale's advocacy of financial and economic reform bore fruit as much as the earnest and persistent pleading of an Indian member of the Viceregal Council of his position and influence could bear it, and the financial statements and the proceedings of that Council bear ample testimony to this fact. In them we clearly see what it was that Mr. Gokhale fought for, what were the directions in which he sought financial progress and what were the aims of his policy. His speeches in the Supreme Legislative Council emphasise certain definite principles which, according to him, ought to have animated the policy of Government, and they are, as it were, so many chapters in a text-book on the financial position and development of India. His views are reiterated, enforced and amplified, from year to year, so that they sink into one's memory on account of repetition of statement, vigour of expression and lucidity of exposition. But he had not the same scope in the Bombay Legislative Council, where the questions he dealt with were of provincial interest and of limited magnitude, though problems like the land revenue policy of the Local Government, supplied him with good material. And before the year 1900, when he became member of the Bombay Council, he had no opportunity to criticise the measures of Government at the same board as the highest resposible officials and thus to ventilate and, in a measure, educate public opinion. His evidence before the Royal Commission on Expenditure in India is indeed a remarkable performance and pointed him out as a leader with great possibilities in him. Before 1897, Mr. Gokhale was, by no means, an unknown quantity in Indian public life, having been already hailed as the rising star of the Deccan. Some of his speeches at and before this time bear the characteristic marks of his genius, but the decade which preceded his appearance before the Welby Commission was a period more or less of preparation, and using the terminology Mr. Gokhale has chosen to describe the members of his Servants of India Society before they are admitted to the full status of membership, we may say that during these ten years he was a leader 'under training.' As he was in no way connected with the work of legislation or the discussion of the Indian budget, we canno get a connected and full view of his ideas about economic and financial reform. And we have to content ourselves with the occasional glimpses we obtain in the speeches he made on the Congress platform and elsewhere.

III. Character of the Times.

The period of Mr. Gokhale's apprenticeship was a period, as we have said above, of a new-born popular enthusiasm and witnessed the agitation for reform started by the National Congress. From the point of view of finance, it was a time of great stress and storm and of additional taxation. Lord Lytton's *regime* was marked by distress caused by widespread famine, by the prosecution of an aggressive military policy on the North-western frontier and by the consequent financial embarrassment, aggravated by a fall in exchange. In 1877-78 famine still raged in southern India. "During the following three years the Government had to meet the heavy expenditure of the Afghan War, which amounted to over 16 crores, exclusive of a contribution made by England, while in 1878–79 there was a further fall in exchange."* For three consecutive years there were heavy deficits. But with the advent of Lord Ripon as Viceroy, came a brief spell of financial prosperity. The revenue jumped up with a bound and when the Provincial settlements were revised in 1882–83, assignments to Provincial Governments were increased and taxation was reduced in the United Provinces at a cost of 24 lakhs. But a wave of deficits and depression came on again and enhancement of the burden of taxation

---

* Imperial Gazetteer of ndia, Vol. IV.

followed. In 1884, the finances were in practical equilibrium, but two of the following four years showed a heavy deficit, and in the remaining two, a small surplus was secured only by the suspension of the famine insurance grant. The Madras famine of 1877 led Lord Lytton's Government to create, by imposing new taxes, a Famine Relief and Insurance Grant. The object of the grant was declared to be the provision of an annual surplus of a crore and a half for famine relief and famine insurance. To the extent to which, in any year the amount was not spent on relief, it was to be spent solely on reduction or avoidance of debt. A pledge was given that the proceeds of the new taxes would not be expended for any other purpose than the one stated. And yet the grant was often suspended for meeting deficits. Lord Dufferin was then Viceroy and the policy of the Government of India as of the Government in England was dictated by the spirit of imperialism. The financial situation of the time is tersely but vividly brought out in the following passage:—"In 1885 occurred the Panjdeh incident on the Russo-Afghan border and the conquest of Upper Burma. The imminent danger of war with Russia involved an outlay on military preparation of two crores, and the Burmese war cost 60 lakhs. In neither case did the matter stop with the initial expenditure. The progress of a great European power towards the borders of India made it necessary to reconsider the military position. The army was increased and larger sums were spent during several years on strategic railways, fortifications, and other works on the frontier. The restoration of order in Upper Burma, and the administration of the Province, also entailed a large net outlay until, after several years, the newly acquired territory began to develop and its revenues to expand. The arrangements so carefully elaborated during Lord Lytton's Viceroyalty broke down under the strain of this accumulated expenditure, and recourse was had to fresh taxation. In January 1886, the license tax was converted into a general tax on non-agricultural incomes in excess of Rs. 500 per annum, and in 1887–88, it was found necessary to enhance the salt duty from Rs. 2 to Rs. 2–8 a maund, and to impose an import duty on petroleum."*

Mr. Gokhale himself gave the Viceroy's Council a brief but graphic description of this financial position in the following words—"During the first 12 years of this period, from 1885–86—when Sir Auckland Colvin told the Council in his financial statement almost in prophetic terms that affairs were 'passing into a new phase', necessitating a reconsideration and revision of the fiscal status established in 1882—down to 1896–97, there was one continued and ceaseless struggle on the part of the Finance Department of the Government of India to maintain, at all risks and hazards a 'strong financial position', in the face of a rapidly changing situation, and provide by anticipation against all possible dangers near and remote, fancied and real;

* Imperial Gazetteer, Vol IV.

and not a year passed—literally speaking—but heralded some change in the financial arrangements of the country. The famine grant was suspended for three successive years, 1886–87—1888–89, then reduced for two more and permanently so in the last year of the period. Twice during these twelve years were the Provincial contracts subjected to drastic revision (1887–88 and 1892–93), and the total gain secured to the Imperial Treasury on such revision and by a contraction of Provincial resources was full 1. 10 crores (64 lakhs in 1887–88 and 46 lakhs in 1892–93). Further more, during the period, thrice (in 1886–87, 1890–91, 1894–95) were the Provincial Administrations called upon to pay special contributions in aid of Imperial revenues. But the chief financial expedient employed to escape the supposed embarrassment of the time was continuous additions to the taxation of the country. Nine years out of these 12 witnessed the imposition of new taxes. First came the income tax in 1886, and then followed in rapid succession the salt duty enhancement of 1887–88 (June, 1888), the petroleum and Patwari-taxes and extension of the income tax to Burma in 1888-89, customs on imported liquors increased in 1889–90, the excise duty on Indian beer in 1890-91, the import duty on salt fish in Burma in 1892-93, the reimposition of the 5 per cent. ad valorem duties on imports, excluding cotton goods, in 1893-94, and the extension of import duties to cotton goods in 1894-95. In 1896 there were changes in the tariff. The 5 per cent. import and excise duties on cotton yarns were abolished and the import duties on cotton goods were reduced from 5 to 3½ per cent.–involving a sacrifice of 50 lakhs of rupees as a concession to the clamour of Manchester, but a countervailing excise of 3½ per cent. was imposed on cotton goods of all counts manufactured in Indian mills." *

This is rather a lengthy extract, but it is calculated to give the reader an excellent idea of the 'time of extreme stress and anxiety' through which India passed towards the close of the last century so far as the finances were concerned, and it was also a time, as has been stated before, when a new spirit and impulse vibrated through the class of educated people in the country. The first session of the National Congress was held in Bombay in December 1885, in the beginning of which year, Mr. Gokhale had joined the Deccan Education ciety, and it was attended, among others, by the late Mr. Ranade, Prof. R. G. Bhandarkar, Principal V. S. Apte and Prof. G. G. Agarkar for all of whom Mr. Gokhale entertained the highest regard during the whole of his life and the last two of whom were his colleagues. This very first Congress passed resolutions on the growth of military expenditure and on fiscal reform and gave a stimulus to the discussion and agitation of public questions. Mr. Gokhale seems to have appeared on the Congress platform for the first time in 1889, and his interest in economic problems began to grow. He became editor of the Quarterly Journal of the Sarvajanik Sabha and

* Budget Speech, 1902.

plunged deeper into public life. Poona had become the centre of remarkable public activities, and the example of Messrs. Ranade and G. V. Joshi, who were devoted students of questions relating to Indian economics and finance and who used to give out to the public the results of their studies, must have inspired and stimulated Mr. Gokhale a great deal. Many of his papers on Indian economics and on the promotion of indigenous industries were written by Mr. Ranade about this time, and in them and in his speeches he brought a fresh, independent and discriminating eye to bear upon the economic condition of India. The stimulating and thoughtful address he delivered at the Deccan College in 1892 on 'Indian Political Economy' has become classical, and Mr. Ranade may be looked upon as the Adam Smith of the Indian school of economic thought. He analysed the political and social situation in India, examined the strong and the weak points of his countrymen and indicated the direction in which salvation lay. At the inaugural address, Mr. Ranade delivered at the first Industrial Conference held in Poona in 1890, he observed :—" We have been all along like most ancient nations, more or less exclusively agricultural. But our contact with the world outside, and the freedom of exchange which has resulted in consequence, have produced one most undesirable result. They have aggravated the situation by making us more than ever dependent upon a single and precarious resource. The industry and commerce of the country, such as it was, is passing out of our hands, and except in the large Presidency towns, the country is fed, clothed, warmed, washed, lighted, helped and comforted generally, by a thousand arts and industries in the manipulation of which its sons have every day a decreasing share. Foreign competition, not because it is foreign, but because it is the competition of nature's powers against man's labour,—it is the competition of organized skill and science against ignorance and idleness,—is transferring the monopoly not only of wealth, but what is more important, of skill, talent, and activity to others.'

IV. The Salt Duty Question.

Such was then the situation when Mr. Gokhale entered upon his apprenticeship to public life. Political and financial reform was in the very air of educated India and he was strongly attracted to economics as a subject to which he might devote special attention. The appointment of the Finance Committee of 1886 was announced by the Viceroy on 4th January of that year in the Imperial Legislative Council. Military operations on the North-West frontier and the continued fall in exchange rendered the financial position most embarrassing. Reduction of expenditure effected in 1885 gave only temporary relief and a thorough-going inquiry into expenditure with a view to the devising of economies, was urged upon Government, and the appointment of the Finance Committee followed. Sir C. A. Elliot was President, and Mr. Ranade was one of its members. The saving, the economies recommended by it, would have effected, could not enable Government, however, to face the financial situation which the conquest and annexation of Burma created. Burma proved the White Elephant of Lord Dufferin's administration, and even the Secretary of State for India had to admit 'that financially, Upper Burma has been so far a disappointment, and he candidly stated that the annexation had 'thrown on' the revenues of India a heavier charge than was expected.' Mr. Westland, the Finance member, was confronted with a deficit of £1½ million and Lord Dufferin's Government decided to fill up this void in the national revenues by enhancing the duty on salt. There were other ways open but they were examined and rejected as unsuitable. It was felt that by economy and retrenchment a sufficiently large saving might have been secured and if that had not been enough, the income tax might have been raised or some tax falling upon those who were able to bear the burden, might have been imposed. In 1886, at the time of the imposition of the income-tax, Sir A. Colvin and Lord Dufferin had pleaded against increasing the burdens of the mass of the population and in favour of taxing the rich and the well-to-do. Assurances had also proceeded from high quarters that there would be no further addition of taxation in India. But in spite of all this, Mr. Westland, the Finance Member, thought that enhancement of the duty on salt was the only practicable and the least objectionable resource of revenue that could be tapped by Government. He said:—" The figures show also that the extra duty of eight annas may be expected to bring in an extra revenue of Rs. 1,60,00,000 and considering the improvement in all means of communication and the generally improved condition of the people, we may reasonably hope that the burden of a duty of Rs. 2-8 will not now have any effect in restricting the rate at which the consumption is increasing."

No tax in India has been more strongly objected to as oppressive to the masses than the duty on salt, which is a necessary of life with the poor man, and the first measure of relief to the tax-payer urged by Mr. Gokhale in Lord Curzon's *regime* of financial prosperity, was the reduction of the duty. The poor man's salt ought to be regarded as an object of taxation only by a desparate Finance Member who has exhausted all other fiscal expedients and is driven by an overwhelming necessity to tax even that necessary of life. When in 1886, the enhancement of the salt duty was proposed as an alternative to the income-tax, Lord Dufferin expressed himself thus :—" The only alternative open to us was to re-enhance the salt tax ; but though this would have been an indirect tax and consequently not so unpopular as the one we are about to impose, its operation would have chiefly affected the poorer masses of the community. Now, I am very far from wishing to say that in the presence of any overwhelming necessity, such as that of a great war, or a great famine, it might not be necessary to raise the duties upon salt." But commercial and other interests were up in arms against any proposal to touch the pockets of the wealthy, and they were indifferent as to the imposition of a burden upon the shoulders of the poorer classes. Before 1892, there were no elected representatives of the people in the Legislative Councils and there were consequently no serious budget debates. The people's view did not find adequate expression in the Councils, and in the case of the enhancement of the salt duty in 1888, even a formal assent of the Viceregal Council was not necessary. The Indian Salt Act of 1882 had empowered the Governor-General in Council to "impose a duty not exceeding Rs. 3 per maund of 82⅔ pounds avoirdupois, on salt manufactured in, or imported into, any part of British India, and to reduce or remit any duty so imposed, and re-impose any duty so reduced or remitted." This clause of the Salt Act conferred upon the Executive Government of the day an extensive and enormous reserve of taxing power under a legislative enactment, by which it can at its own will and pleasure at a moment's notice add to its current revenues no less a sum than full 3½ crores without further application to the Legislature for sanction to that addition."*

Armed with this power, the Executive Government notified the public on January 19th, of their having raised the duty on salt and later on, though not bound to do so, Mr. Westland referred to the question in his speech in the Legislative Council, in the course of the discussion on the taxing bills before

* Rao Bahadur G. V. Joshi's Writings and Speeches.

it. In his paper on The Burma Deficit and the Enhancement of the Salt Duties, Mr. Joshi wrote:— "But even a deficit of nearly 2 millions now as is the estimate, is a very serious affair for a poor country like India. Optimistic writers in the press assure us that the Government of Lord Dufferin need not be appalled by this crisis. The course adopted by Government, however, is that of working along the line of least resistance. They dare not touch the import duties, because of the British clamour it would raise; they dare not ask the English Government to bear part of the expenditure incurred to keep forward English interests; they will not reduce expenditure lest the services rebel; they therefore come down upon the silent millions who cannot speak and levy a poll tax of 2 annas per head by raising the duty 25 per cent. upon the cost of manufacturing salt! In the exercise of the powers vested in it under the Salt Act of 1882, section 7, Government has thought fit by a Notification in the *Gazette of India Extraordinary* to raise that duty on salt from Rs. 2 to Rs. 2-8 in continental India and from 3 annas to Re. 1 in Burmah, making thereby a sudden permanent addition at a moment's notice of nearly two crores to its annual revenue." It is superfluous to add that this measure created great commotion and dissatisfaction in the country, and a reduction of the salt duty was pressed upon the attention of Government from year to year, till they thought it fit to grant the relief in 1903 when surpluses in the overflowing treasury left no excuse for withholding the reform.

V. *Appearance on the Public Platform.*

At the Calcutta Congress of 1890, Mr. Gokhale spoke in support of a resolution pleading a reduction of the duty on salt, and he briefly but clearly brought out the points in favour of the measure noticed above. He said:—"I say that the measure for the enhancement of the duty on salt in January, 1888, by a mere executive order of the Government of India was a cruel departure—I might almost say a criminal departure from the wise policy long since laid down by the Government of India and reaffirmed, strange as it may seem, when Lord Lytton was our Viceroy and Sir John Strachey our Finance Minister, namely the policy of raising a revenue from salt by a low rate of duty and unrestricted consumption instead of by a high rate of duty and restricted consumption. I say that this new departure was extremely unjust, that as a measure of statesmanship it was extremely impolitic and that its consequences have been simply disastrous." Mr. Gokhale went on to demonstrate the truth of this statement, and in a touching peroration, drew a vivid picture of the misery of the mass of the people affected by the enhancement of the salt duty. Already in 1889, Mr. Gokhale had made a speech at the Bombay Congress in seconding the fifth resolution voicing the popular dissatisfaction created by the orders of the Secretary of State for India on the re-

port of the Public Services Commission. The document was extremely disappointing and the Secretary of State's orders were more disappointing still. This subject has an economic as well as a political aspect, and the employment of Indians in the higher services cf the country has been urged as much on financial grounds as on those of justice and expediency. But we have only to call the attention of our reader here to the systematic manner and lucidity of Mr. Gokhale's exposition of every topic he handled. These qualities of his bespeak the care with which Mr. Gokhale studied and thought out problems to himself. There is no confusion of ideas and no vagueness. Precision and pointedness were the characteristic features of the facts and arguments marshalled, which came one after another in their orderly array. As an example we give here an extract from the above speech. Said Mr. Gokhale:—
"I had intended to review the whole question but time is short and I am afraid of abusing the almost fatherly indulgence of the President. My point is two-fold. First, that the Commission, which was appointed with such a flourish of trumpets, left us in a worse position a great deal than did the Commission's report. I want to draw your attention to three points. First, there were competitive examinations before the Commission sat and before the Secretary of State issued his orders. Secondly, there was the statutory system whereby one sixth of the posts reserved by the enactment of 1861 for the Covenanted Service were to be given to Indians.

Thirdly, what is called the Provincial Service or the Uncovenanted Service, was theoretically at least almost exclusively ours, the natives of India. With regard to these three points, let me tell you what the Commission did and what the Secretary of State has done."

To the great misfortune of the country, Mr. Gokhale did not live to see the completion of the work of the Islington Commission on the Public Services, of which he was a prominent member. He had carefully studied the whole question and gave expression to his views on the public platform from time to time. Another problem to the solution of which he so passionately devoted himself, later on, seems to have engaged Mr. Gokhale's attention at an early date and it was the problem of mass education. His campaign against illiteracy will ever remain a memorial of the earnestness and persistence with which he fought for reform. Speaking in support of the eighth resolution in the Congress of 1891, deprecating a diminution of educational grants and advocating an inquiry into the industrial condition of the country, Mr. Gokhale observed:-"India is the least advanced in the matter of education. I have statistics with me but will not quote them. You will find that in the countries of Europe, 90 per cent. of the school-going population attend school ; but in our own country the proportion is only 11 per cent. I have also statistics with regard to expenditure ; but I will mention only a few. In Europe, in the most backward country as far as education is concerned, no less than 6·5 per cent. of the public revenues goes towards the expenses of education, whereas in India the proportion is about 1 per cent." The intimate relation between education and national progress made such a profound impression on Mr. Gokhale's mind that, towards the close of his public career, he bent all his energies to the question of free and compulsory education, and it was always an important plank in his programme of reform. The seven or eight years preceding his appearance before the Welby Commission in 1897, we have somewhat arbitrarily characterised as a period of Mr. Gokhale's apprenticeship to public life. The Commission recorded very valuable evidence, though it narrowed the scope of its inquiry against the declared intentions of those who appointed it. Before proceeding to unfold the financial and economic situation and needs of India as reflected in that evidence and the case for reform made out by Mr. Gokhale and the other Indian witnesses as also by the writers of the minority report, it is necessary to give the reader an idea of the general position of affairs in this country.

VI. Falling Exchange.

These last ten years constitute a period of transition in the history of Indian finance as in the story of Mr. Gokhale's life-work. They were years of heavy deficits, of a falling exchange, a dwindling opium revenue and of two of the most disastrous famines that have ever occurred in India. The decade which succeeded these years of anxiety and depression, viz. the beginning of the present century, found exchange established upon a firm basis, the treasury of the Government of India over-flowing with continuous surpluses and the State in a position to undertake new schemes of expenditure and to remit taxation. The forward policy on the frontier entailed heavy non-recurring and recurring expenditure and increased the serious difficulty which falling exchange and decreasing opium receipts had created. The deficits had to be met by the imposition of additional taxation and even the resumption of a portion of the growing revenues of the Provincial Governments. The total gross revenue of India and the total expenditure charged against revenue, for the ten years, 1890-1900, are shown in the following table :—

Year.	Gross Revenue.	Gross Expenditure.
1890-91	85,74,16,440	82,05,34,780
1891-92	89,14,32,830	88,67,57,480
1892-93	96,17,24,380	91,00,58,500
1893-94	90,56,52,140	92,11,22,120
1894-95	95,18,74,290	94,49,43,190
1895-96	98,37,01,670	96,83,61,690
1896-97	94,12,97,410	95,83,47,630
1897-98	96,44,20,040	101,80,12,150
1898-99	101,42,66,930	97,46,53,830
1899-1900	102,95,57,460	98,79,38,110

As to opium receipts, which have now become practically extinct, they had been steadily declining in the last quarter of the nineteenth century. In 1876-7 opium yielded 16 per cent., and in 1902-3 only 7 per cent., of the total net revenue. But the cause of the greatest disturbance and anxiety in Indian finance was the continuous fall in the gold value of the silver rupee and the consequent increased amounts which the Government of India had to find to meet the 'home charges.' Exchange fell since 1883-84 from 19·536 d to 13·0 d per rupee in 1895-96, and the loss on Home remittances increased in consequence from Rs. 3,37,37,000 to Rs. 13,11,63,000 —a net increase of about 9½ crores. To make this point clearer it may be mentioned that in 1873-74, before the fall in the exchange value of the rupee commenced, the amount of Home remittance, in lieu of payments the Secretary of State makes in England, on behalf of the Indian Government, of such charges as interest on debt raised in England, civil and military pensions, salaries, the price of stores &c. was about £ 13 millions, which at a rate of exchange of 1 s. 10·351 d., was represented by Rs. 14,26,57,000. During 1892-93, the amount remitted was £ 16½ millions which, at the average rate of exchange in that year, viz 1 s. 2·985 d., required a payment of Rs. 26,47,84,150. If this could have been remitted at the rate of exchange of the year 1873-74, it would have needed only Rs. 17,75,19,200, which means that there was a loss of Rs. 8,72,64,950 entailed upon India by the falling exchange in that year.

VII. The Currency System.

It is necessary to state here that before the gold value of the rupee was fixed at 16 d., there was great uncertainty as regards the amount which the Government of India had to remit to the Secretary of State from year to year. The Indian revenues are raised in silver rupees and the foreign remittances have to be made in gold. The lower the gold value of silver, therefore, the higher the amount which the Indian Government must spend for meeting the home charges. In fact, the drop of one penny in this exchange value added more than one crore to the amount of rupees that had to be provided for procuring the necessary amount of gold to meet the home charges in England. It is by means of bills of exchange, which the Secretary of State sells to British importers of Indian goods, who have to make remittances to this country, that he draws the funds needed to meet the home charges, and this method dates from an early part of the last century. Down to 1872-73, the rate of exchange at which the Secretary of State was able to sell his drafts upon the Indian treasuries, did not fall much below 2 s. the rupee. There began then a decline which continued down to the end of the century. In 16 out of the 27 years ending in 1898-99, the Secretary of State was unable to realize the budgeted amount of home charges. The downward movement of the gold value of silver began with the demonetisation of the white metal by Germany after the Franco-German War. The metal thus discarded found its way to America and India, whose currency systems stood upon a silver basis. By the Bland Act of 1878 and the Sherman Act of 1890 it was made compulsory for the American Government to make large purchases of silver with a view to raising its value, and yet the metal fell from 52½ d. per ounce, the average of 1878 to 43½ d. in 1890 and later on to 37½. The continuous fall in exchange was the cause of extreme embarrassment to the Government of India, as we have pointed out above, and there was no prospect of improvement. The deficits which the falling exchange combined with military and other expenditure to cause from year to year, were met by the imposition of fresh taxation and the limits of the tax-paying capacity of the people seemed to have been reached. The unsteady, uncertain and fluctuating tendency of the exchange imparted to trade the character of gambling and speculation, and merchants loudly complained against that evil as much as European officials who had to make remittances abroad. An agitation was started by people interested in a steady and high exchange rate against the existing currency system and they urged immediate reform upon the attention of Government.

As early as 1876, the Bengal Chamber of Commerce and the Calcutta Trades Association, alarmed at the fall in the value of silver, memorialized the Viceroy, urging the temporary suspension of the compulsory coinage of silver by the Indian mints. The Government of India was not at that time disposed to view the proposal with favour. They declared that 'a sound system of currency must be automatic or self-regulating' and decided that 'up to the present there is no sufficient ground for interfering with the standard of value'. But their growing difficulties made the Government change their mind and they addressed a despatch to the Secretary of State in 1878, suggesting, among other things, the introduction of a gold standard and gold currency into India and the limitation of the free coinage of silver in the Indian mints. The proposals were, however, stoutly opposed by the Lords Commissioners of the British Treasury to whom they had been referred for opinion, and they stated that the relief to the Indian Government, and to civil servants and other Englishmen remitting money to England, which, it was supposed, would attend the adoption of the proposals, would 'be given at the expense of the Indian tax-payer and with the effect of increasing every debt or fixed payment in India including debts due by ryots to money-lenders'. Writing to the India Office, in 1886, the Treasury observed :—" It is impossible to regard this question from the point of view either of the Indian exchequer or of the Anglo-Indian official without a corresponding regard to the general effect of the fall in the gold price of silver upon the trade and prosperity of the great mass of the population." The Treasury seem to have 'accepted the general belief that the fall of the rupee was rather to the advantage of Indian manufactures'.* The continuous fall of the rupee, however, at last induced the British

* R. C. Dutt.

Government to depart from the policy it had so long maintained on behalf of the Indian tax-payer and the Indian industries. The question of the Indian currency was therefore referred to a Committee presided over by Lord Herschell, then Lord Chancellor, and they were asked to consider whether, having regard to the difficulties which confronted the Government of India through the heavy fall in the price of silver, it was expedient for His Majesty's Government to allow them to stop the free coinage of silver. From the evidence that came before it, the Committee concluded that the evil complained of as to the effect of a falling exchange was genuine, that economy, though derirable as a remedy, was impossible and that the limits of taxation in India had been reached. The Committee reported in 1893 in favour of the closing of the mints and an Act was accordingly passed immediately, stopping the mints in the face of the free coinage of silver.

The chief complaint against this measure was that it sacrificed the interests of the Indian people to the clamour of a small section of self-interested agitators and that the true remedy lay in retrenchment and economy and not in a tampering with an automatic system of currency. "A hue and cry was raised throughout India when the announcement regarding the closure of the mints was made by Government. Men of experience and acquaintance with local conditions vehemently protested against the measure and characterised it as a death-blow to the Indian export trade. But during the long number of years that have intervened, the people of India have been thoroughly accustomed to the change and the trade has not only recovered any set-back which it may have temporarily sustained at the time but has, since, made rapid strides."* This view is now largely shared in India, and critics of the currency policy of Government have reconciled themselves to the change of 1893 as it has undergone still further developments and is not likely to be reversed. The main object of the closing of the mints was to make rupees scarce and thus to enhance their price by rendering impossible their competition with the Secretary of State's drafts on the Indian Government. This object of artificially raising the value of the rupee was attained forthwith, and it rose steadily from 13·1 d. per rupee in 1894-95 to 16·0 d. in 1898-99. Now the Government of India wished that the policy of 1893 should be carried to its logical conclusion, that the gold value of the rupee should be permanently fixed and that a gold standard should be adopted. The Secretary of State, therefore, appointed another Committee, with Sir Henry Fowler as chairman, to deliberate and report upon the monetary system in force in India. Though such witnesses as Sir Robert Giffin strongly objected to the artificial system set up in India and recommended economy and the reduction of certain heavy charges which were unfairly imposed upon this country, as cures of its currency ills, the Committee did not open the question of general policy. Sir Henry Fowler's

* Currency Organizations in India by Mr. Alakh Dhari.

Committee submitted its report in 1899 and recommended that the British sovereign should be made a legal tender and a current coin at the rate of 1s.4d. per rupee and that without undertaking to give gold for rupees at that rate, Government should accummulate a gold reserve out of the profits they would receive on the coinage of rupees owing to the difference between the intrinsic and the face value of the silver token, and that this gold should be made available for foreign remittances when a fall of exchange made such help necessary. Thus the policy of a gold standard and a gold currency was definitely laid down and accepted by the Government of India. How far it was carried out in practice and what were its financial and economic effects we shall discuss in a later chapter.

VIII. *The Cotton Duties.*

Before the Mutiny there was a general import duty of 5 per cent. on all commodities coming into the country. It was raised during the next few years in view of the heavy expenditure the Government had to meet. But very soon the tendency commenced towards lowering of the tariff so that by the beginning of the last quarter of the nineteenth century the import duties stood at 5 per cent. About this time, however, 'the question of abolishing the customs duties began to be discussed. The Government of India desired to give the fullest play to free trade principles, and the Lancashire cotton manufacturers finding a serious competitor in the growing Indian industry, were pressing for the removal of the artificial advantage given to the latter by the 5 per cent. duty ' ! * The House of Commons pressed, at the instance of Lancashire manufacturers, a resolution in 1877 to the effect " that, in the opinion of this House, the duties now levied upon cotton manufactures imported into India, being protective in their nature, are contrary to sound commercial policy, and ought to be repealed without delay, as soon as the financial condition of India will permit." Lord Salisbury, who was then the Secretary of State, pressed upon the Indian Government the urgency of a repeal of the import duties on cotton goods and yarn on the ground that they had a protective effect, and Lord Lytton's Government was prepared to submit to all demands unconditionally, though they were strongly opposed by high officials and the public in India. In 1878 and 1879 certain duties on cotton imports, which were supposed to have an unfavourable effect upon the Lancashire industry, were removed. " The duty was actually repealed when Southern India had not yet recovered from the Madras famine of 1878; when new cesses on land had recently been added to the land revenue; when the Famine Insurance Fund created by special taxes had disappeared; when the estimated budget showed a deficit; and when troubles and a vast expenditure in Afghanistan, brought about in quest of a scientific frontier, were impending."† It was not wise to have sacrificed a large source of revenue, especially at a time of falling

* Imperial Gazetteer, Vol IV. † R. C. Dutt.

exchange, recurring famines and growing military expenditure. When, under Lord Ripon, however, financial prosperity temporarily returned, the Government abolished the remaining import duties in 1882 in a fit of generosity. For the twelve years 1882—1894, no fresh import duties were levied, except a small duty on petroleum in 1888. But the falling exchange and rising military expenditure once more forced Government to resort to fresh taxation. In 1894 they were confronted with a deficit of about two crores, and as other methods of filling up the void were considered as impracticable, (the Herschell Committee having pointed to the customs as the only source available) a duty of 5 per cent. *ad valorem* was imposed generally on all articles with a few exceptions. Cotton yarns and fabrics were, of course, exempted to satisfy the free trade conscience and Lancashire interests. To the outcry that arose against this measure Lord Elgin, in passing the Tariff Act in March 1894, threw out a hint that it was not a final arrangement. In December of the same year, a fresh Act was passed subjecting cotton fabrics and yarns to a 5 per cent. duty, but propitiating Manchester, at the same time, by imposing a countervailing excise duty of 5 per cent. upon yarns produced in Indian mills which, it was thought, would compete unfairly with those of Lancashire. The British manufacturing interests were not, however, satisfied and they clamoured for more favours. Lord George Hamilton who had, on the accession of the Conservatives to power in 1895, become Secretary of State for India, urged the Indian Government to modify the tariff so as to leave Lancashire no ground for complaint. Lord Elgin's Government accordingly introduced into the Viceregal Council, next year, the Indian Tariff Amendment Bill and the Cotton Duties Bill, which imposed a 3½ per cent. duty on all woven goods and exempted all yarns, but which still subjected all cotton goods produced in Indian mills to a 3½ per cent duty. The measure met with strong opposition from all sides and was condemned by officials and non-officials, Europeans and Indians. Twenty years have passed since then and the outcry against the iniquitous excise duties has been hard and persistent. 'As an instance of fiscal injustice the Indian Act of 1896 is unexampled in any civilized country in modern times.' The excise duty remains as a lamentable memorial of the subordination of Indian interests to those of Lancashire and of the fiscal dependence of the Government of India on the will of the Secretary of State whose policy is swayed by extraneous considerations and exploded theories.

IX. The Famines.

After having enjoyed comparative immunity from any serious famines for about eighteen years, India had, in 1896 and again in the last year of the Nineteenth century, to pass through the ordeal the severest that had ever been sent to her to try her patience and staying power. The last calamity, in particular, was very wide spread and caused enormous distress. Government's machinery of famine relief was severely tried and the famine taught the State many a lesson in administration. The first of the two famines of this decade "occurred in 1896-97 during Lord Elgin's administration and was chiefly felt in the United Provinces, the Central Provinces, Behar, Bengal and portions of the Punjab. In the Central Provinces the difficulties of famine relief were very great and the famine operations were, on the whole, defective. A Famine Commission was afterwards appointed under the presidency of Sir James Lyall and its report had just been prepared when Lord Curzon landed."* The second calamity which overtook the country three years later, was more widely spread and caused greater havoc. Lord Curzon, who had toured round the famine-stricken parts and seen the distress with his own eyes, summed up some of the features of the famine in the following words :—" It was not only a crop failure, but a fodder famine on an enormous scale followed in many parts by a positive destruction of cattle—both plough cattle, buffaloes and milch kine. In other words, it affected and may almost be said to have annihilated, the working capital of the agricultural classes. It struck some of them when they were still down from the effects of the recent shock. It struck others who had never before known what calamity was and who were crushed and shattered by the suddenness and directness of the blow......For a

*" India Under Curzon and After " by Lovat Fraser.

year it never left hold of its victims and one half of the year had not elapsed before famine had brought its familiar attendant furies in its train, and cholera, dysentery and fever had fallen upon an already exhausted, enfeebled population. This is the picture of suffering that India has presented during the past year." The loss of human life and of cattle, due to this famine, was enormous and the cost to Government and the Native States for providing direct relief and for remission of land revenue was extremely heavy. As we have remarked above, the famines taught Government many a lesson as to their causes and their cure and also as to the proper organization of relief. Measures for prevention and treatment were gradually developed in the light of experience and of the recommendations of the Famine Commissions. But before the close of the last century, the famine policy and measures of the State gave cause for serious criticism and in supporting, at the Calcutta Congress of 1896, a resolution appealing to the Government to apply the Famine Insurance Fund more largely to the immediate relief of the famine-stricken people, Mr. Gokhale said :—"There was a time when Government held that it was no part of its duty to bring relief to the distressed people, and that the Government would leave the natural economic laws to work out their own relief. Happily, however, that time has long passed, and the Government has now made the fullest and amplest admission of its responsibilities." He then proceeded to pass a scathing criticism on the inadequate and unsatisfactory character of the relief measures taken by Government in his own Presidency and the hardships which those who received relief had to suffer. "These poor creatures," he said, "have fled from starvation and death these poor creatures are starved also on the relief works and when complaints of their treatment are made to the Government, they are coolly told that if they are not satisfied they may complain to their superior officers, or if they prefer it, leave the work." At the time of the famine of 1877, an appeal for assistance had been made to British charity and had received a noble response, bringing about a crore of rupees into this country from England. A similar appeal on the occurrence of the last great calamity of the century was equally fruitful. But Mr. Gokhale emphasised the importance of charity beginning at home and appealed to his countrymen, rich and poor, high and low, to "come forward to bring help and consolation in order that as many lives as possible might be saved and in order that the evil effects of the famine might be averted as far as possible." Fortunately for us, India has not been overtaken by calamities of this terrible type during the past fifteen years, though scarcity, in one part of the country or another, is ever with us. Famine relief machinery has likewise greatly improved and both government and people have come to realize their responsibilities in the matter. Organization of private relief to supplement the efforts of

Government has been found necessary and has proved very beneficial. And it may be noted that the members of Mr. Gokhale's Servants of India Society have taken a commendable part in the organization of this kind of relief.

X. Home Charges and 'Drain' Theory.

There is one very important subject which requires notice before we bring the present chapter to a close, and it is the much-misunderstood and misrepresented question of what has become famous as 'drain'. Mr. Dadabhai Naoroji persistently hammered at this subject and advocated such administrative and economic reforms as would tend to stop what he called the material and moral drain to England. It indeed betrays a lamentable lack of the knowledge of the laws of Political Economy to suppose that a country which exports more than it imports and which borrows capital in foreign countries, or pays highly the services of foreign experts it employs, is in a parlous state and is bound to go to ruin. Some such notions seem to lie at the bottom of the criticism of those who maintain that all the payments which are made abroad on behalf of India for interest on the capital borrowed, for civil and military salaries and pensions and for the stores purchased, constitute a drain of her wealth and are, as such responsible for her economic decadence. These payments are not gratuitous and are made for benefits received. If we want railways for the development of the resources of the country and cannot raise the necessary capital, we must borrow it in London where it is obtainable at cheap rates. We want an army and a navy for the defence of the country and must pay for it. Foreign countries and the self-governing colonies borrow very largely in the London market and cheerfully bear the charge of interest. It is foreign capital that has made the economic development of these countries possible, and payments for services received cannot be characterised as a tribute. These considerations ought to be borne in mind by those who indiscriminately condemn the Home Charges as a drain of India's wealth, and the fact that the blessings of British rule cannot be had for nothing and that no country can escape the payment of a value equivalent to the advantages enjoyed, must not be lost sight of.

If this is the misconception of the charges India pays in England on the one side, there is on the other side, an equally serious apprehension of the position of those who advocate the reduction of such charges on the ground that they stunt the material and moral development of the people. Taking up the material aspect of the question, it must be stated that borrowed capital invested in railways and irrigation works, is certainly a beneficent factor in the production of wealth. And it ought to be freely admitted that European experts have to be imported and highly paid too. But the aim of the policy of the State ought to be to train the people themselves so that the charges paid by India may turn out a really good investment. For several years to come, we shall require the services of experts of various kinds for our development. Our effort must, however, be to substitute Indian agency in the place of the foreign agency in all departments. The British Government has so often declared it to be the aim of its policy to prepare the people to govern themselves and generally to bring them up to the British standard. The demand of the Indian people that the high civil and military posts should be thrown open to them, especially now that they have demonstrated their capacity, whenever opportunities have been given to them, is based upon this principle, and not only will Home Charges be reduced if this reform is introduced but the moral development of the people will likewise be stimulated. If the growth of indigenous industries is similarly promoted by the State wealth, production in India will increase and the profits which at present go out of the country, will remain to fructify in the pockets of the people and to form the store of capital necessary to build up nascent industries. Mr. Dadabhai Naoroji and others have never fallen victims to the fallacy that India's trade with foreign countries is detrimental to her prosperity. On the contrary, they have contended that the larger the wealth produced by the people, the larger will be their imports of foreign goods and the happier will they be. That is why they have insisted upon the desirability of the accumulation of capital in the country and the more extended employment of Indians in the public service. The analogy of foreign countries and the Colonies which borrow in London, is misleading in as much as they pay only interest upon their loans but retain all the profits. This India is not able to do and much of the wealth produced in the country goes out in one form or another. The prayer of the people to Government, therefore, is that they should equip the country in such a way that it will be enabled to manufacture its own raw materials, accumulate more capital and promote its material welfare. There is a well-founded complaint* that the administration of India is very costly and if the reforms suggested are carried out, there will be a great saving to the immense benefit of the people.

Latterly a good deal of improvement is visible in the attitude of Government; but it is extremely and unjustifiably slow. As regards the public services Mr. Dadabhai says :—" Beyond the positions of Deputy Collectors or Extra Commissioners, or similar subordinate positions in the Engineering, Medical, and all other services (with a very few somewhat better exceptions), all experience and knowledge of statesmanship, of administration or legislation, of high scientific or learned professions, are drained away to England, when the persons possessing them give up their service and retire to England."§ These exceptions, it must be frankly admitted, are now-a-days becoming more frequent, but there is absolutely no justification for the hesita-

* See an interesting article on this subject in the January number of the Modern *Review* from the pen of Lala Lajpat Rai.

§ The Poverty of India.

tion and caution. Mr. Dadabhai, who was a member of the Welbey Commission, brought out the material aspect of the problem we are considering, in his cross-examination of Mr. Gokhale. The question at issue was the extreme dependence of the people upon land and the decay of Indians industries. Mr. Gokhale stated that there was a universal feeling in the country that protection was the remedy for the economic decadence. He was asked why the Indian people did not start new industries. The following questions and answers followed :—

(Mr. Naoroji) What is the reason they were not able to take up these industries such as teao r any of these industries, or any of these enterprises which the foreigners came and took possession of ? Is it not because our capital is carried away from the country ?:—Yes, that is so.

Is not that at the root of the whole thing ?—Yes ; it is at the root of the whole thing.

If that were not so, and we were able to preserve what we produce we should be able to welcome the foreigners to do what they liked and we should be able to compete on equal grounds with them ?—Yes, exactly.

Otherwise we are reduced to be mere labourers, hewers of wood and drawers of water; whereas now, of the profits of all these new improvements and trades and manufactures introduced into the country nothing remains ; those profits are all taken away by somebody else ?—Yes.

This helplessness of the people is indeed undergoing a change for the better and Indian enterprise and Indian capital are forthcoming in a larger measure than eighteen years ago. That does not, however, affect the principle under discussion. The economic transition through which India is passing is undoubtedly responsible for the unsatisfactory condition of things in this country, and periods of transition have at all times and in all countries, entailed great hardships. But a thoughtful writer makes the following remarks in connection with Prof. Lees Smith's observation that 'India's great danger is inertia and that the resources of the country are not being opened up by Indian initiative.*' He says:—" The truth of the economic generalisations is obvious enough. But the lack of initiative on the part of the people is the natural outcome of the disappearance of their means of livelihood. It is a misconception of the doctrine of the survival of the fittest merely to view with complaisance the deaths of those that succumb. It is a misconception of the doctrine of free trade merely to refuse to regulate industrial development. A bureaucracy may not be eminently suited to inspire enthusiasm; but it can exaggerate its fear of producing inertia. It has at least peculiar opportunities for assisting, for teaching and for protecting."§ Sweeping generalisations are often mischievous ; so is the one in

---

* India and the Tariff Problem.

§ The History and Economics of Indian Famines-by A. Loveday.

connection with the Drain. But there is an equally great danger in the desperate attempts sometimes made to maintain the *status quo* and to refuse to budge an inch. The truth lies midway between the two extreme positions and we believe we have been able to bring it out above.

When the position is thus made clear so far as the fundamental principle involved in the question is concerned, it will not require much effort to make out a convincing case in favour of the reduction of the Home Charges that is being advocated from year to year. At a largely attended public meeting of the inhabitants of Bombay held in July, 1893, under the presidentship of the late Sir Pherozeshah Mehta to adopt a memorial to the House of Commons on the subject of the Home Military charges in India, Mr. Gokhale made a notable speech, in which he pointed out how Viceroys and Secretaries of State for India had, one after another protested against these charges as excessive and unjust. He showed with the help of statistics how the burden thrown upon India's shoulders by the War Office on account of the British forces in this country, had grown very heavy and moved the adoption of a memorial praying that the burden might be reduced and the money overdrawn by England be refunded to India. Lord Northbrook had raised a debate on this question in Parliament and at the Lahore Congress of 1893, Mr. Gokhale proposed a resolution rendering thanks to his Lordship for his noble endeavours to reduce the Home charges and praying the House of Commons to appoint a committee to settle the matter. The equitable division of certain charges between Great Britain and India, in matters in which both are interested, was a subject for enquiry before the Welby Commission. The substitution of Indian agency, in the place of European, in the administration of this country on the ground of economy, justice and expediency, is being constantly pressed on the attention of Government; and the urgency of the State taking comprehensive measures to promote the material and moral development of the people, so that they may be as efficient, self-reliant and prosperous as their fellow-subjects in the other parts of the Empire, is as patent to-day as it ever was.

CHAPTER II.

THE ORDEAL.

I. The Welby Commission.

The account, given in the last chapter, of the development of Indian finance during the closing decade of the last century, must have conveyed to the reader a fairly good idea of the growing expenditure of the Government of India and the ever-increasing burden of taxation thrown on the shoulders of the people. The heavy cost of the military operations carried on and beyond the frontiers of India had been imposed upon this country and there was a strong feeling in India and in England that the administration was extravagant and the people were unnecessarilly saddled with expenses which, in justice, should have been borne by the British Exchequer. Inquiries were often made and economies suggested. But they bore no fruit and things went from bad to worse. Mr. Dadabhai Naoroji had long been working hard in England to impress on the attention of the British public and the Parliament the growing poverty of India, the costly character of the administration and the sense of injustice felt in this country at the treatment accorded to its people. He appealed to the liberal and liberty-loving instincts of the British race, to the pledges given in statutes and Royal proclamations and the pronouncements made by British statesmen as to the policy which was to govern the administration of India. He demanded the fulfilment of the pledges given to the Indian people and pleaded for political and economic reforms which were calculated to render India prosperous and happy and make it an important asset of the British Empire. Selfless and untiring, he devoted many years to the advocacy of the cause of India in England and he was the first Indian member of the British Parliament, having been elected to the House of Commons by his constituency in Central Finsbury, in the year 1892. In Parliament, as outside it, Mr. Dadabhai was active in his advocacy of India's cause and in his maiden speech in the House of Commons he observed:—" So long as India is satisfied with the justice and honour of Britain, so long will her Indian Empire last and I have not the least doubt that though our progress may be slow and we may at times meet with disappointments, if we persevere, whatever justice we ask in reason we shall get." He sincerely believed that ' there is a great and glorious future for Britain and India to an extent unconceivable at present, if the British people will awaken to their duty, will be true to their British instincts of fair play and justice, and will insist upon the 'faithful and conscientious fulfilment of all their great and solemn promises and pledges.'* Mr. Dadabhai continued with the perseverance so characteristic of him, to press for reforms and financial justice

*The Poverty of India by Mr. Dadabhai Naoroji.

for India, in the House of Commons and his strenuous labours resulted in the appointment of a Royal Commission in 1895 with instructions "to inquire into the administration and management of the military and civil expenditure incurred under the authority of the Secretary of State for India in Council or of the Governor of India and apportionment, of charges between the Governments of the United Kingdom and of India for purposes in which both are interested." Lord Welby was the President of the Commission, and among its members were Sir William Wedderburn, Mr. William S. Caine and Mr. Dadabhai Naoroji himself.

These last three gentlemen disagreed with their colleagues as to the views and recommendations of the majority of the Commission and they submitted their own report. In it they complained that the majority was inclined to restrict the scope of inquiry to the merely technical action of the machinery of Indian administration and the settlement of the disputes between the Secretary of State for India and the British War Office. But the minority report complained, the Secretary of State had distinctly said in the House of Commons in 1894 that the scope of the inquiry was to be wider and the Commission was to inquire whether the machinery of British administration in India had produced prosperity in the country and whether India was better or worse for being a province of the British Crown. Though the Commission narrowed the scope of their inquiry and made it purely mechanical and though they thought they were not concerned with such fundamental questions, which really mattered, as, the spirit of British rule in India and its economic and financial effects upon the people of this country, the evidence it recorded was extremely valuable, the witnesses who appeared before it being some of the most distinguished administrators and financiers who had been connected with India. The Indian point of view was also placed before the Commission by the Indian witnesses, Messrs. Wacha, Surendranath Banerjea, Gokhale and others, and the report of the Commission and its appendices form a most instructive record for the student of Indian finance. There he gets a fine review of the development of the machinery of Indian administration, and of the economic condition of the Indian people and he is enabled to form an opinion of the character of the reforms which are called for in the interest of progress. Much water has flowed under the bridges since the report of the Commission was published, but it has much more than a merely antiquarian interest for the present generation. In spite of the reforms which the last fifteen years have witnessed, the political and financial organization of India yet stands in need of a comprehensive readjustment, almost an overhauling, and the hopes which the war has given rise to, points to the urgency of such bold steps being taken in the direction of progress. Most of the serious faults in the governmental machinery against which Indian people complained fifteen years ago are still there and the programme of reform which was urged by Indian witnesses before the Welby Commission has a peculiar interest at this moment when the air is full of discussions as to the political and fiscal readjustments that will have to be made in the interest of India on the restoration of peace.

The writers of the minority report of the Welby Commission complained not only at the narrow view which their colleagues had taken of the scope and purpose of their instructions, but also of the scant attention they had paid to the case as seen from the Indian point of view. The Commission having decided to call, at the public expense, three non-official Indian witnesses from Calcutta, Madras and Bombay, the authorities in India secured for this important duty the services of gentlemen well-qualified to speak on behalf of Indian public opinion. Messrs. Surendranath Banerjea, G. Subramani Iyer and D. E. Wacha were these representatives. Mr. Gokhale went in addition, as the representative of the Deccan Sabha. Public meetings in Calcutta and elsewhere deputed Dr. K. N. Bahadurji M. D. to give evidence on the subject of the Indian Medical Service. Mr. Dadabhai Naoroji, an indefatigable and earnest member of the Commission, also gave evidence, as also Mr. Margon Brown, late Secretary to the British Committee of the Indian National Congress. The minority report regrets that the Commission as a whole did not give to the evidence of these gentlemen, who could present India's case more faithfully than the other witnesses, the importance it deserved and the report of the majority contains no reference to the facts and views put forward by Mr. Dadabhai and the other Indian witnesses. These latter were subjected to a hot fire of cross-examination but they stood the test most successfully. Mr. Gokhale was the youngest of the whole lot ; but he had prepared his case very carefully and equipped himself completely. Mr. G. V. Joshi, whose knowledge of administrative and economic problems was almost unsurpassed by any Indian, gave valuable assistance to Mr. Gokhale who had also the blessing of Mr. Justice Ranade. The Guru who took a paternal interest in the young Professor from Fergusson College, was anxious that his pupil should acquit himself creditably before the commission and the writer of this book remembers with what ardent curiousty and interest he read the accounts of Mr. Gokhale's cross-examination as they appeared in the newspapers. The young witness must have trembled with diffidence as he stood before the veteran Commissioners, sending volleys of inconvenient and tricky questions. But the youthful hero faced the attack boldly and calmly, and Mr. Ranade was highly gratified with his performance. In fact, the manner in which Mr. Gokhale presented his case and maintained his position in the face of a severe cross-examination, extorted universal admiration and at once brought him to the front as one of India's ablest politicians and economists.

II. Minority Report.

The Commission decided to divide its work into three parts and to devote its attention to three different issues viz. (1) the machinery of financial control, (2) the growth of expenditure and (3) apportionment of charges between England and India. On the first point it came to the conclusion that the financial machinery was well organised that its action was effectively controlled. It compared the British and Indian systems and pointed out how the latter was slow moving and suffered for certain drawbacks, one of which would be removed if the financial year were changed to obviate revised estimates. The comparative methods of collecting revenue and disbursement were gone into and the relations of the Finance Member to the Viceroy and the Secretary of State as well as his powers were examined. The Commission found a drawback here and a drawback there, but was on the whole, satisfied with the machinery and its working. In England the auditors of the nation's accounts are independent of the Executive Government, but on the question of rendering the Indian Auditor and Comptroller General equally independent, the Commission was divided, the change being opposed by the Government of India on the score of expense. The Commission, however, inclined to the view that Indian accounts should each year be laid before Parliament after being examined by an independent committee. On the second point, the Commission entered on an elaborate inquiry into the growth of expenditure.

For this purpose it started with the year 1861-62 and the period between that year and 1895-96, it divided into two parts, the first one of 23 years (1861-62 to 1884-85) and the second covering 11 years (1884-85 to 1895-96). By manipulating figures the Commission endeavoured to arrive at the normal growth of tax revenue and the normal growth of expenditure. And it came to the conclusion that the increase of revenue had been great in proportion to the growth of population and that but for the heavy loss entailed by unfavourable exchange, the revenue had been larger than the expenditure and even provided a balance for the reduction of expenditure. The Commission's findings were similar as to the public debt, the cost of the collection of revenue and the apportionment of charges between England and India. On the cost point, they recommended a small relief to the Indian treasury out of the British Exchequer.

A minority of Commissioners, consisting, as stated above, of Sir W. Wedderburn, Mr. Caine and Mr. Dadabhai, disagreed with the majority on certain fundamental points and disapproved several of their recommendations. They stated that the inquiry of the Commission into the growth of expenditure was most perfunctory and that it had accepted the conclusions of the official witnesses. Additional burdens which weighed heavily upon the people, such as the enhancement of land revenue and so forth, had not been taken into calculation and therefore the figures given in the report were vitiated. Again, the attempt of the Commission to arrive at normal expenditure was futile, as India, not being a self-governing country, there could be no natural adjustment in its case between expenditure and public needs. The people had no voice in the sanctioning of the expenditure and the raising of revenue and real and urgent needs of the country were not met for want of funds. Under these abnormal conditions the test applied by the majority of commissioners was falacious. As to the apportionment of charges between England and India they had unnecessarily restricted the scope of inquiry to a few minor matters. Mr. Dadabhai who had protested against this procedure, was not heeded to and no importance was attached to his evidence as that of other Indian witnesses. The minority report emphasised the acknowledged poverty of the people and the impossibility of taxing them further. Salvation therefore lay in economy and retrenchment and this could be achieved largely by the substitution of Indian agency in the place of the existing costly European agency. Simultaneous examinations approved by a committee of the India Office in 1860 and by a resolution of the House of Commons in 1893, must be instituted, and the solemn pledges given by the Crown and various statutes such as the Act of 1833, must be fulfilled. A larger employment of Indians in the civil and military services would be productive of economy, efficiency and good government.

Coming to the heads of the inquiry, the report stated that there was no effective check upon the Government of India. An independent audit like the one proposed would be no advantage as the House of Commons did not vote the Indian budget. The Viceroy was all powerful and the Finance Member could exercise little influence. The restraint of the non-official members of the Viceroy's Legislative Council was nominal and the India Council also was unable to exercise any check. The House of Commons took little interest in Indian affairs and the side of the Indian tax-payer was not placed before Parliament. The ministry therefore suggested that the House of Commons should appoint a committee to scrutinise the financial condition of India. It recommended that (1) the non-official members of the Viceregal Council should be made more directly representative of the people, that (2) the Council should vote the budget and that (3) Indians should be nominated to the India Council. We have referred above to the opinion of the dissenting minority that the method, adopted by the Commission, of arriving at the growth of revenue and expenditure was faulty and that its conclusions were therefore unwarranted. While opium revenue was regarded as tax-revenue, land revenue was not. Exchange steadily improved after the year 1895 and it was ludicrous that a report published in 1900 should put down conclusions based on figures prior to the year 1895. A prominent feature of the period reviewed by the Commission was a heavy increase in military expenditure. A change in frontier policy began in 1885 at the close of Lord Ripon's administration and costly military expeditions and works were undertaken. Military expenditure of a special character amounted, during a period of ten years from 1885 to 1895, to $47\frac{1}{2}$ crores of rupees. Heavy sterling liabilities were incurred and the exchange compensation allowance threw a large burden upon the shoulders of tax-payers.

Proceeding to consider the position of Provincial finance, the minority report drew pointed attention to the fact that a lion's share of the revenues of our country was absorbed by the Imperial Government. The Provinces did not enjoy financial independence and there was no stability or continuity in their financial arrangements. A sense of responsibility was not developed in the Provincial Governments and the original object of decentralising finance was frustrated. The minority therefore recommended a scheme, which had been put forward by certain members of the Finance Committee under which there would be no divided heads, which would be either wholly Imperial or wholly Provincial. The sum by which Imperial expenditure exceeded Imperial revenue was to be a first charge upon Provincial revenues. Provincial surpluses were to provide for Imperial deficits before increased expenditure could be undertaken by Provincial Governments. Lastly, future growth of revenue was to be equally divided between the Imperial and Provincial Governments. As to the apportionment of charges between England and

India, they should be equitably divided as between two partners and not as between a master and dependant. The three commissioners concluded by clearly indicating the defects of the existing financial management and suggesting remedies. We do not reiterate these, as they may be easily gleaned from their views we have summarised above. It is needless to say that the report of the Welby Commission caused disappointment in India. Its recommendations were not calculated to give much relief to this country and the main object of its inquiry, so far as Indian public opinion was concerned, was not attained. "On the other hand, the really larger questions of reduction of the Indian debt, reduction of the Home Charges and of taxation and reduction of the military expenditure remained untouched. The duty of relieving the Indian tax-payer of the burden of a heavy and excessive taxation remained unfulfilled. The problem of bringing to the lives of the two hundred millions of British subjects in India something of that comfort and prosperity, which are the heritage of British subjects elsewhere in the world, remained unsolved.*

III. Gokhale's Case.

Speaking in the name of the people of India, though primarily a representative of the Deccan Sabha, Mr. Gokhale put in his case in a clear, concise and convincing manner so that no amount hickling to which he was exposed could materially shake him from the strong position he had taken up.

* R. C. Dutt.

Mr. Gokhale maintained that the machinery of financial control in this country was most defective, owing to the fact that while in the United Kingdom and the Colonies public expenditure is administered under the control of the tax-payers and therefore presumably solely in the interests of the tax-payers, in India other interests are often deemed to be quite of equal importance and are sometimes allowed to take precedence of the interests of the Indian people. 'Thus we have, first of all, the standing claims of the interests of British Supremacy, entailing a vast amount of expenditure, the benefit of which goes to others than the tax-payers of the country.' The large European Army maintained on a war footing in time of peace, the practical monopoly of nearly all the higher offices in the Civil services by Europeans and the entire monopoly of such offices in the Native Army are illustrations of this statement. We have next the interests of the extension of British dominion in the East, large sums having been spent from time to time in the past for this purpose out of the Indian exchequer, in many instances, in spite of the protests of the Government of India. It is not only the interests of the European civil and military services but those of British commerce and of British commercial and moneyed classes that often prevail over the interests of India. The frequent subordination of Indian interest to other interests, contended Mr. Gokhale, made it all the more imperative that the machinery of constitutional control should provide adequate safe-guards for a just and economical administration of the Indian expenditure but it was a matter of regret that nowhere were the safe-guards more illusory than in the case of India. The spending authorities in the matter of Indian expenditure are (1) the local Governments, (2) the Government of India and (3) the Secretary of State in Council. The controlling authorities are the Government of India, controlling the Provincial Governments, the Secretary of the State controlling the Government of India and the Parliament, in theory, controlling all. This is all, however, official control, and real popular control in the sense of control by tax-payers is practically speaking, absent from the whole system. The right of moving resolutions in connection with the budgets has indeed been granted by the Morley-Minto reforms, but it does not go far as the budgets have not to be passed by the Legislative Councils. Parliament exercises little control over the Secretary of State for India and therefore over Indian expenditure and the protection which the vigilance of Parliament used to accord in the time of the East India Company, is no longer available to us. 'The position virtually amounts to this, that it is the administration of the finances of one country by the executive government of another, under no sense of responsibility to those whose finances are so administered.' As a result, millions upon millions have been spent on objects which have not advanced the welfare of the Indian people in the least while measures which alone could have secured the true well-being and prosperity of the people have been woefully neglected.

The whole position may thus be summed up in the words of Mr. Gokhale:—

(1) The buffer of the company's Government, which fairly, pretected Indian interests, is gone, and there is no effectual substitute.

(2) We have no effective constitutional safeguards against the misapplication of our revenues for extra-Indian requirements.

(3) The control vested in the Council of the Secretary of State under the Statute of 1868 is rendered almost nugatory by the alterations of its status under recent Amending Acts.

(4) The control of Parliament, as against the Secretary of State has become entirely nominal, owing to the latter being a member of the Imperial Executive, with a standing majority behind him. The old periodical inquiry by Parliament and its jealous watchfulness are gone. In fact we have at present the disadvantages of Parliamentary Government without its advantages. In the case of our Departments except the Indian, ex-Ministers think it their duty, and also feel it to be their interest, to exercise the closest watch on the proceedings of their successors with a view to passing the most adverse criticism that may be possible. In regard to India alone ex-Ministers vie with and some times even go beyond their successors in extolling all that exists and all that is done. The responsible Opposition in this country thus abdicates its functions in the case of India only.

(5) The Government of India, as at present constituted, cannot be much interested in economy. Almost all internal administration having been made over to Local Governments under the Decentralization. Scheme, questions of foreign policy, large public works, and military questions absorb almost the whole attention of the Government of India. Further, the Finance Minister excepted, every other member of Council including, since 1885, the Viceroy, has a direct interest in the increase of expenditure.

(6) Neither in England nor in India is there the salutary check of public opinion on the financial administration. Parliament is ill-informed and even indifferent. And the Supreme and Local Legislative.

Councils are simply powerless to control expenditure, since budgets have not to be passed and no resolutions with reference to them can be moved.

Mr. Gokhale was not content with indicating the defects of financial machinery of India and suggested remedies, the (1) first of which was that the Indian budget should be passed item, by item in the Viceregal Legislative Council, Government retaining their standing majority and thus having an absolute guarantee that no adverse vote would be carried against them. This will now be regarded as a very moderate demand and an inadequate reform, when a majority of elected members in the Legislative Councils and the power of the purse are being pressed for on behalf of the people. (2) The second suggestion had reference to a Committee of control to be established in England which was to have no powers of initiating expenditure but was to take cognizance of all appeals addressed to it by the non-official members of the Viceroy's Council and might also call for papers of its own accord and exercise general control over the administration of Indian expenditure. The plan did not, in any way, affect the directive and executive powers of the Secretary of State or the Government of India, but provided only for a reasonable amount of control and was calculated to enable the representatives of Indian tax-payers, who have no powers of controlling expenditure, to make a complaint in a responsible and constitutional manner. (3) The third remedy lay in an amendment of Section 55 of the

Act of 1858 which enacted that "except for preventing or repelling actual invasion of Her Majesty's Indian possessions, or under other sudden and urgent necessity, the revenues of India shall not, without the consent of both Houses of Parliament, be applicable to defray the expenses of any military operation carried on beyond the external possessions of such frontiers by Her Majesty's forces charged upon such revenues." Now, this clause provided a guarantee for the sanction of Parliament for the division of India's moneys from their legitimate use, but it did not give us a complete guarantee against the misappropriation of Indian revenues for purposes unconnected with India's interests. As in the case of the expeditionary forces placed at the disposal of His Majesty's Government by India in the struggle with German barbarism, expenditure of Indian revenues may be most willingly voted for expeditions beyond the frontiers but under normal conditions, Mr. Gokhale insisted on a statutory provision that, except in case of an actual or threatened invasion, those revenues should not be used for operations beyond the natural frontiers of India (these being once for all defined), unless, at any rate, a part of such expenditure was put on the English estimates. (4) The fourth remedy was the investing the elected members of the Provincial Legislative Councils with the power to return to the Imperial Parliament one member for each Province. Here Mr. Gokhale had no delusions as to the actual results likely to be directly achieved by these half-a-dozen Indian representatives in a House of Commons of 670 members but he relied more upon the moral effect of the cause proposed than upon any actual results. (5) The last suggestion was "that as far as possible, Indian Viceroys should be selected from among men who have earned a distinct position for themselves for their grasp of intricate problems of finance." The connection of the Viceroy with the Foreign Department, it was urged, led to extravagant military expenditure and it was suggested that that Department should be entrusted to a separate member of the Executive Council. These reforms would be regarded in these times as extremely modest and it must be remembered that they were suggested eighteen years ago when the political horizon of India was obviously limited and the popular imagination had not yet learned to take bold flights in the higher regions of constitutional development. But modest as they were, it took more than eleven years and much painful experience for some of the suggestions to be considered as worthy of serious consideration.

IV. Provincial Finance.

The Provincial Governments have no powers of independent taxation. They collect revenue in their territories for the Supreme Government and are allowed to retain a certain portion thereof for meeting the share of expenditure for which the Provincial Governments are responsible. Certain heads of revenue are absolutely assigned to these

Governments, the revenue from certain heads is shared by them with the Imperial Government, while other heads are entirely Imperial. Receipts from most of the spending departments are taken by the Provincial Governments. These financial arrangements were made semi-permanent in 1904 and the final stamp of permanence was placed upon them seven years later. Before that, at the end of every five years, the Government of India made contracts with the Local Governments on the basis of the existing financial conditions and they were quinquennially renewed. Every time the contract was renewed, the Government of India tried to improve its own position by taking a slice of the Provincial revenues and leaving the Local Governments to better their financial situation by economy or in other ways. There was thus an element of uncertainty in the whole position and the Provincial Governments were, by no means, pleased with the Supreme Government swooping down upon their savings every time the contracts were revised. These Governments therefore became indifferent to economy and extravagant, and fought among themselves and with the Government of India for a larger share of revenue. Before 1871, all financial authority was centralised in the Supreme Government, and the Local Governments were merely agents collecting revenue for the higher body and expending what was given to them to meet provincial charges. They had therefore no interest in economy and stimulus to reform. Lord Mayo initiated the measure of decentralisation in finance, and handed over to Local Governments certain charges along with receipts from those specified heads, the excess of Provincial expenditure over Provincial revenue being made good by lump assignments from the Supreme Goverment. Lord Mayo expected that his scheme of decentralisation would lead to (1) economy, (2) increased responsibility on the part of Local Governments, (3) avoidance of administrative difficulties and (4) the institution of local self-government tending to associate the people with the rulers in the conduct of public affairs. As local taxation was more convenient, and the national expenditure was growing, the Provincial Governments were to be left to improve their financial position by economy and taxation. Municipalities and local bodies have been allowed to raise funds by means of rates, but the Provincial Governments have been denied the power to levy taxation on their own account, independently of the Supreme Government.

The financial embarrassments of the Government of India, in the first instance, suggested the idea of decentralization as a means of relief to the national exchequer, and no opportunity was lost to add to the resources of the Imperial Government even at the cost of the Provincial Governments. This was justified on the ground of the heavy responsibility which lay upon the Supreme Government for the defence and efficient administration of the country. Foreign policy, defence and the railways were in its hands, and these costly charges were reflected in its constant financial difficulties. Lord Mayo's

If the Provincial Governments and the people do not want the existing system, the Government of India cannot long continue to resist the demand for financial reorganization. Decentralization of power will have to take place and the Local Governments will have to be invested with powers of taxation. The present financial arrangements fit in well with the idea entertained by the Central Government of its own authority and responsibility. But it is the Provincial Governments who come in closer contact with the people and are called upon every day to face urgent problems of expansion and improvement. Their resources must, therefore, be more elastic and more amenable to their own control. The existing arrangements will, therefore, have to go and be replaced by others more in consonance with the needs and demands of the people. This is the essence of the reform Mr. Gokhale advocated and in spite of the developments the system of Provincial finance has undergone during the last few years, never was the desire for Provincial autonomy keener than it is at the present day. The new historical Despatch of the Government of India, of the 25th of August, 1911, has stimulated and strengthened the hopes of the people as to this autonomy and no one would be more pleased to have it than the Provincial Governments themselves. That Despatch said that 'the only possible solution of the difficulty would appear to be gradually to give the provinces a larger measure of self-government, until at last India would consist of a number of administrations

calculated to place the Indian financial system once for all on a sound basis and to bring it more in a line with the federal systems of finance in other countries such as Germany, Switzerland, Canada and the United States. The Minority Report endorsed this proposal and taking the figures for revenue of the year 1895-96, showed how the lion's share was taken by the Government of India! The following are the figures :—

1895-96.

Net Revenue under Principal Heads.

	Crores of Rs.		Percentage.
Imperial Share ...	43	...	69
Provincial Share ...	19	...	31
	—		—
Total ...	62		100

If the cost of collection were deducted the shares would be 74 : 26. This question of overhauling the financial arrangements between the Government of India and the Provincial Governments, cannot be brushed aside as being a subject of merely academic interest and we hope and believe that it will be earnestly taken up at the first opportunity. Finance Members have not received the idea with favour and the Hon'ble Sir Guy Fleetwood Wilson has expressed the view that though opinions may differ as to the ideal system of dividing revenue between the Imperial and Local Governments, there can be no question of over-throwing a system long established and steadily developed.*

* Financial Statement, 1911-12.

Dufferin s Finance Committee of whom Mr. Ranade was one. They proposed :—

(1) That there be no divided Departments, but that those Departments of receipts and expenditure which are now wholly, or almost wholly Imperial, or which it may be found convenient to make Imperial, should be set on one side for Imperial purposes, and that the receipts and expenditure of the provincialised departments should be entirely Provincial.

(2) That whatever the sum by which the Imperial expenditure exceeds the income from those sources of revenue which are not provincialised, that sum should be declared the first charge on the Provincial revenues.

(3) That the Provincial surplus which arises from the excess of receipts over expenditure should be the fund from which, in the first place, all Imperial necessities should be met before any increase can take place in Provincial expenditure.

(4) And that as regards the future growth of revenue, it should, as far as possible, be divided equally between Provincial and Imperial, subject to the condition that if the Imperial exigencies ever required a larger share, the Imperial share should be increased.

This scheme is calculated to safeguard the interests of the Provincial Governments while making ample provision for the necessities of the Central Government, at the same time imposing something like a check on its spending propensities. It is

In 1897, the system of Provincial finance, as described above, still prevailed, and Mr. Gokhale characterised the contracts as 'really one-sided arrangements practically forced on the weak Provincial Governments by the Government of India, which is all powerful in the matter.' We have remarked above that it was the financial embarrassment and evergrowing expenditure of the Supreme Government which led it to make these contracts, at the revision of which large amounts of Provincial revenue were often resumed by the Government. Thus taking Bombay we find that in 1886-87, the last year of the contract of 1882, its expenditure was about 4 crores, which had to be reduced by about 18 lakhs in 1887-88, the first year of the next contract, and it was not till 1891-92 that the level of 1886-87 was again reached, when at the next revision, it was again put back. It was admitted from the outset that the contracts were not based upon any fixed or intelligible principle. There was no uniformity in their plan and they did not impose equal burdens on the different Provinces. Another defect Mr. Gokhale pointed out in the existing system was that while it operated as a check on the growth of Provincial expenditure, it imposed no similar restraint upon the spending propensities of the Government of India. He approved of the remedy recommended by four members of Lord

crease which had taken place in the cost of the army to a searching analysis and examination and proved how the burden was too much for the shoulders of the people who did not secure a commensurate benefit therefrom. The army was too large for the needs of India and too costly for its capacity. It entailed heavy annual expenditure which prevented Indian revenues from being devoted to measures of material and moral progess.

Besides the financial loss involved in the whole system, Mr. Gokhale emphasised the moral loss also. This was a point which be never ceased to hammer because with it is bound up the elevation of the Indian people to the status of other races. The goal of British rule in this country, can be no other than the raising of India to the height of the other members of the Empire and the aspirations and efforts of the people have always been directed to the attainment of that goal. Mr. Gokhale's words are worth quoting :— "The excessive costliness of the foreign agency is not, however, its only evil. There is a moral evil which, if any thing, is even greater. A kind of dwarfing or stunting of the Indian race is going on under the present system. We must live all the days of our life in an atmosphere of inferiority, and the tallest of us must bend, in order that the exigencies of the existing system may be satisfied. The upward impulse, if I may use such an expression, which every school boy at Eton or Harrow may feel, that he may one day be a Gladstone, a Nelson

autonomous in all provincial affairs with the Government of India above them, and possessing powers to interfere in case of mismanagement.' This kind of decentralization will be useless, it is superfluous to point out, unless it is accompanied by the concession of an adequate measure of popular control over the Provincial administrations.

V. Progress of Expenditure.

The enormous increase which had taken place in the expenditure of India was the main subject to the investigation of which the labours of the Welby Commission were addressed. The phenomenon of an unprecedented expansion of national expenditure is a feature of recent years in almost all western countries and the mere increase, taken by itself, is not necessarily open to any serious objection. But as Mr. Gokhale was very careful in pointing out, 'while increased expenditure in other countries, under proper popular control, has, so far as we are able to judge, helped to bring increased strength and security to the nations, and increased enlightenment and prosperity to the people, our continually growing expenditure has, in our opinion, under autocratic management, defective constitutional control, and the inherent defects of alien domination, only helped to bring about a constantly increasing exploitatio of our resources, has retarded our material progress weakened our natural defences and burdened us, with undefined and indefinable financial liabilities.' He then went on to trace the growth of expenditure on various heads and subjected the enormous in-

ture over provincialised receipts, a certain proportion of the Imperial revenue of each province is, for the future, to be devoted to this object. Thus certain heads of revenue were reserved as (1) wholly Imperial, (2) others were divided between the Supreme Government and the Provincial Governments mostly equally and (3) the rest were wholly Provincial. The balance of revenues and charges thus made Provincial, being against the Local Governments, was to be rectified for each of them by a fixed percentage on land revenue otherwise reserved as imperial. The advantage of the new system was declared to be that Provincial Governments would be given a direct interest not only in provincialised revenue but also in the most important item of Imperial revenue raised within their Province.* This was certainly an advance upon the old arrangements but the system has never given any satisfaction except to the Government of India. With the modifications introduced into the system of contracts in 1904 and in 1911, we shall deal at a later stage. Suffice it here to state that even to-day the Provincial Governments, at any rate, public opinion in the Provinces wants a radical reform and Provincial Autonomy in the matter of finance is being urged. Provinces feel that they are unjustly or illiberally treated and they would have liberty to order their financial house according to their needs and capacity.

* See Government of India's Resolution, 30th September, 1881.

scheme was further developed in 1877 and 1882 with the object of giving the Provincial Governments greater interest in economy and improved administration. The sources of revenue placed at their disposal were extremely inelastic and hardly capable of expansion. The weak point in the arrangements of 1871 was that while the charges transferred to the Local Governments had a tendency to grow, the revenue transferred, though not quite fixed, had little room for development. It was, therefore, decided to apply the system of Provincial assignments of 1871 to revenue also. What was intended was not giving the Provincial Governments power of local taxation to enable them to expand their resources but to offer them direct inducements to improve those sources of existing revenue which depended for their productiveness upon good management. In the time of Lord Lytton, further heads of expenditure including, in most Provinces, land revenue, general administration and law and justice, were transferred to local management and in addition to the allotment of a lump sum, the Imperial Government likewise transferred to the Provincial Governments the entire receipts under certain heads of revenue, reserving to itself a share in the prospective increase. When the quinquennial contracts came to be revised in 1882, a new principle was adopted in the financial settlements made with the Provinces. Instead of giving Local Governments, as heretofore, a fixed sum of money to make good any excess of provincialised expendi-

or a Wellington, and which may draw forth the best efforts of which he is capable, is denied to us. The full height to which our manhood is capable of rising can never be reached by us under the present system. The moral elevation which every self-governing people feel cannot be felt by us. Our administrative and military talents must gradually disappear, owing to sheer disuse till at last our lot, as hewers of wood and drawers of water in our own country, is stereotyped." It will be apparent from this how financial reform was associated in Mr. Gokhale's mind with the moral and material progress of the Indian people. The appointment of Indians to high and responsible public offices in their own country is a question of paramount importance even to-day and the significance of the above-quoted sentences has come to be deeper than ever.

The grant of exchange compensation allowance to all non-domiciled European and Eurasian employees of Government about the middle of 1893, oused in this country a storm of disapproval and Mr. Gokhale's contention that it was an unnecessary and wasteful measure was supported with strong arguments. 'While the miserable pittance spent by the Government on the education of the people' he said, 'has stood absolutely stationary for the last five years on the ground that Government has no more money to spare for it, here is a sum larger than the whole educational expenditure of Government given away to its European officials by one stroke of the pen !'. The meagerness of the Government assistance to public education in India, was, according to him, one of the gravest blots on the administration of Indian expenditure and he reiterated his plea that it should be wiped off, to the last days of his life. The subject of education, primary education in particular, was ever dear to Mr. Gokhale's heart and referring to the Bombay Presidency he observed that 'so long as we have only 9,000 public primary schools for over 25,000 towns and villages, and about 80 children out of every 100 of school-going age are growing up in utter darkness, so long the educational policy of the Government will always be a reproach to it' And he suggested that Local Boards whose revenue is small and almost fixed, should be empowered to levy special educational cesses, if they pleased.

As to the apportionment of charges between England and India, Mr. Gokhale pleaded, in the first place, that in strict justice, the India Office ought to form part of the Imperial Establishments and paid out of the Imperial Exchequer as the salary of the Colonial Secretary, together with his office charges, is borne on the Imperial Estimates. In view of the much directive and executive work in regard to Indian administration which the India Office has to do, he would be satisfied if the charges were divided half and half between India and England. He likewise contended that the thirty thousand troops that were added to the Army establishment of India mainly as an Imperial Garrison and as an Imperial reserve, ought to be paid out of the Imperial treasury. Turning to the Ordinary Public Debt of India, as distinguished from the Public Works or Productive Debt of India, it was pointed out that the bulk of it represented 'charges unjustly imposed on us' in the past in respect of various wars and expeditions in promotion of Imperial schemes of territorial expansion. From calculations it was found that a total amount of 114-6 crores was unjustly imposed on India by the Imperial Government in furtherance of its own policy. It is interesting to note that Mr. Gokhale mentioned the fact that 'we have paid every shilling of the cost of the British conquest' including even the cost of the suppression of the Mutiny, England 'having contributed absolutely nothing in aid of all this expenditure', while she paid such charges for Imperial conquest or settlement in respect of her Colonies. All political expenditure beyond the Frontier, he contended, ought to be borne on the Imperial Estimates, as India has no interests whatever beyond her territorial borders and has only to maintain peace and order on her own side of the frontier.

VI. The Cross-Examination.

On the principal points in his written evidence, Mr. Gokhale was cross-examined at great length and though he was subjected to volleys of searching questions, he stuck to his guns all right. The Commission was not able to shake him from his position with regard to the absence of any effective check upon the administration of India, the defective constitution of the India Council which had neither Indians nor independent Englishmen upon it and the absolutely nominal character of the control which the Parliament is supposed to exercise upon the Secretary of State. It is well-known that in Parliament every member is regarded as 'a member for India', and the Opposition is practically non-existent so far as measures relating to India brought forward by the ministers are concerned. This peculiarity of Parliamentary Government in connection with India was clearly brought out when he observed :—"In the case of all departments except the Indian, ex-Ministers think it their duty and also feel it to be their interest to exercise the closest watch on the proceedings of their successors with a view to passing the most adverse criticism that may be possible. In regard to India alone, ex-Ministers vie with and sometimes even go beyond their successors extolling all that exists and all that is done. The responsible Opposition in this country thus abdicates its functions in the case of India only". Who does not know that the Opposition is awakened to a sense of its duty only when the politicians in power that is, the Secretary of State for India proposes reforms which public opinion in this country urgently demands ?

As we have remarked above, the cross-examination went on along the lines of the written evidence which has been already summarised, and it gave Mr. Gokhale an opportunity to explain his views satisfactorily and reinforce them with facts, figures and arguments. It is not necessary to go over that ground again though the cross-examination makes very interesting and instructive study, but we shall content ourselves with referring to certain points raised by Mr. Gokhale which appeared to the Commissioners as very extraordinary and on which therefore they exposed him to a hot fire of questions. One of such questions was his remark that 'a constantly increasing exploitation of our resources retarded our material progress.' The railway policy of Government has, no doubt, opened up the country and the improved means of communication have provided a safeguard against famines. The food grains and raw materials of India are being exported in larger quantities on account of the railways having penetrated the interior of the country and the cultivator is getting larger return from his land. But against these obvious advantages must be set the disadvantages of railway construction which has been pushed on with extraordinary vigour, which are not so easily perceived. While bringing into the country the cheap products of Western factories and taking out raw materials in return for them, the railways have killed all indigenous industries and driven the artisans and craftsmen on to the land. This is the objection—which would otherwise appear silly—which has been taken to the almost feverish haste with which the programme of railway construction was prosecuted. On this question the following passage-at-arms occurred:—

"Then you would prefer to have gone without the railways all the time; your idea of improving the material prosperity of India would have been to have adopted none of these improvements such as rail-roads which most people think tend to develop a country?

"Well, I am not quite so sweeping in my assertion. I do not mean that the railways themselves are to be condemned—all the railways —but the manner in which the Government are going in for more and more railways, starving more useful things, is our objection; and this has resulted in the exploitation of our resources by the indigo, tea, coffee, and other planters. The policy of freetrade has, moreover, been forced upon us too early, thereby destroying all our important industries existing before, and throwing all the people on the precarious resource of agriculture. . . .

"Will you tell us how the making of rail-roads has retarded your material progress, because you say "that the increasing exploitation of our resources has retarded our material progress"?
——"Well, this free trade policy that has been thrust on the country has killed all our industries. No colony has accepted this policy. The result is that our people are growing poorer and poorer, because they are all thrust back on agriculture. Sir James Caird, in his report, says that there are so many idlers now connected with land; I believe half the number would do the argricultural work; and the other half are kept on land because they have nothing else to do; and the result is so much labour is practically idle there; and the old industries that we had are swept away under the competition of steam and machinery; so that has retarded our progress."

"Then the opening of fresh trades must have the opposite effect, must it not?—But that is very little; we get only wages there, and every thing else goes out."

There was then a very lively exchange of observations on the questions of India's poverty, the supposed relation between the imports of the precious metals and growing prosperity, the increasing army expenditure and the organization of famine relief. The question of the expansion of railway communication was once more referred to, and Mr. Gokhale stated it as his deliberate opinion that no money should be spent upon the extension of railway lines until other and more urgent needs of the country had been satisfied. It must be borne in mind that railways in those days, were a losing concern and the bulk of the capital sunk in them was borrowed abroad. Even to-day, the people of India do not approve of crores of rupees being borrowed every year for prosecuting an ambitious programme of railways, whose management is not sympathetic and does not directly benefit them in a way they may be calculated to do. The construction of branch and feeder lines is indeed desired and does draw capital out of the people, but railways which simply transport raw material to the big ports and convey into the interior of the country manufactured goods imported from foreign countries, are not regarded as beneficial. Mr. Gokhale's views on this question seem to have proved very unpalatable to most members of the Commission. We give below a few typical questions and answers:—

"(Sir William Wedderburn) Looking to the very difficult position of Indian finance, you think that railways are a luxury for which the country can wait a little though they do desire them?—That is my view; that is also Sir Auckland Colvin's view.

(Chairman) Would you really impress it on the Commission that the Secretary of State and the Government of India have undertaken these railways principally in the interests of English commerce and commercial monied classes; is that a direct charge of yours?—That is the impression in India because the facts are there. Whenever a Viceroy goes out to India there is a deputation that waits on him, and they put pressure on him to construct these railways, and he makes a promise, more or less, that he will do his best. There is no feeling in India that there should be these railways—the Finance Member is opposed to them. The Finance Commission recommenned that 20,000 miles of railways would be practically sufficient, so far as protection from famine was concerned—that total has been reached, and still there is a new programme of 28 crores.

(Sir William Wedderburn.) Has any great native Association, like the Indian National Congress, ever pressed for that rapid extension o railway communications?—Never.

In the 12 years in which they have made representations to Government, that has not been included in their programme ?—Never.

Therefore you assume that it has not been owing to Indian pressure that this activity has gone on ?—Yes. That is my view.

Often has such criticism been heard outside and inside the Viceroy's Legislative Council even during the last few years and the utterances of Finance Members, weighed with a proper sense of the financial responsibility involved, leave no doubt in one's mind as to the pressure sought to be brought upon them by certain interests and the difficulty experienced by them in bearing it. Adverting to the opinion held in some quarters that the remunerative character of our railways was beyond question, that our railways were the milch cow of the Government of India and that the Finance Member was ungrateful, Sir Guy Fleetwood Wilson solemnly remarked :—"Let me remind you that so recently as in 1908-09 our railway system was worked at a net loss to the State. I said at the time that we must never allow our railways to become again, even temporarily, a net burden on the general tax-payer. I repeat that assertion. As matters stand, we have in our railways a splendid asset. Let us safeguard that asset. Any admission of doubtful schemes, or failure to count in each case the full cost, any disregard of financial considerations, will surely lead to deterioration of a most serious character."*

* Speech introducing the Financial Statement for 1913-14.

Another subject which attracted particular attention was that of the Famine Insurance Fund. As we have already stated, Lord Lytton's Government created the Famine Insurance grant by imposing additional taxation, the object declared being the provision of an annual surplus of a crore and a half for famine relief and famine insurance. It was authoritatively stated that this annual grant thus provided from extra taxation was not to be devoted to any purpose other than the one stated. Sir James Peile, one of the Commissioners, contended that the Acts which imposed the new taxes never referred to any sacred Famine Fund and that the words of a law must be considered as a higher authority than the words of the Secretary of State for India or any one else. The Chairman also maintained that what a statesman said twenty years ago about a certain charge being necessary, could not be binding for all time. And he quoted the words of Sir John Strachey, the Finance Member used in explaining the bill which imposed additional taxes for providing the Famine Fund, suggesting the possibility, at a future date, of the special provision being diverted to other purposes or reduced or suspended. Mr. Gokhale, in reply, took his stand on the declarations made by the Secretary of State as to the object, character and scope of the Famine Fund.. He stated that his complaint was two-fold. 'First of all, they have been paying interest out of the fund which was repeatedly declared to be an entire inversion of the fund; secondly, when they first diverted the fund to other purposes, they never made an express declaration that they were so doing, which they were bound to make in view of the pledges which they had given before.'

VII. Defects and Remedies.

It will not be uninstructive if we note here briefly the defects which the writers of the Minority Report found in the existing financial management and the remedies they suggested for their removal. They were of opinion that (A) Indian expenditure was not governed by Indian considerations and this defect was reflected in (i) the Frontier Policy, (ii) the extension of railways without due regard to other and more urgent needs, and (iii) continued special concessions to European officials. They maintained that a greater part of the recent increase in expenditure was on these heads. (B) It was further noticed that due care was not taken in spending Indian money and this statement was illustrated by reference to the facts that (i) qualified Indian agency was not substituted for European agency, (ii) controlling and supervising agencies had grown beyond proper limits, (iii) Indian armies were maintained on a permanent war footing, (iv) the number of British troops was disproportionately large (v) employment of Indians in the army was restricted and (vi) the policy in connection with railway contracts and concessions was not satisfactory. (C) Another defect pointed out was the faulty distribution of expenditure, and the fault lay in (i) more being spent on so-called national defence and less on national development; (iv) Imperial expenditure being much larger than the Provincial and (iii) more being expended on the improvement of communications than upon the improvement of the condition and capacity of the people. As regards apportionment of charges between Great Britain and India, the Minority Report observed that the apportionment should be as between two partners and not as between master and slave.

CHAPTER III.

INITIATION.

I. Lord Curzon.

It was no easy task to take the place of Sir (then Mr.) Pherozeshah Mehta in the Supreme Legislative Council which Mr. Gokhale did in 1902 when that sturdy patriot retired and found room for his young countryman in that august body. Mr. Gokhale was there placed in a situation of very great responsibility and difficulty. The Legislative Councils did not, at that time, give much scope for the show of ability or the performance of constructive work of national utility, to non-official members. But Mr. Mehta had established high traditions in the Viceroy's Council, traditions of independence of judgment, frankness of utterance, display of debating powers and well-informed and courageous criticism of the policy and measures of Government. His powerful speeches in the Council and his advocacy of the cause of his countrymen were universally admired and his services were gratefully acknowledged by the public in Calcutta, Bombay and elsewhere. Mr. Pherozeshah was a dreadful opponent as the highest officials often found to their cost. His intellectual and debating powers were unrivalled and his ways were inimitable. Mr. Gokhale was called upon to succeed him and showed in a few years that the choice was not mistaken. Mr. Mehta had already had opportunities to form an opinion of the young aspirant's abilities, and his speeches in the Bombay Legislative Council and on the platform outside as also his evidence before the Welby Commission had marked him out as the coming leader of India.

The commencement of this century was to be rendered memorable by the Viceroyalty of Lord Curzon than whom no more brilliant, more ambitious, more industrious, more efficient, more capable and more eloquent British politician had been sent out to shape the destinies of this land. Many have attempted to form an estimate of his character and career and we have some very interesting portraits of the Viceroy presented to our view. We have one from Mr. Gokhale himself who speaks of that pro-consul thus :—" In some respects his Lordship will always be recognised as one of the greatest Englishmen that ever came out to this country. His wonderful intellectual gifts, his brilliant powers of expression, his phenominal energy, his boundless enthusiasm for work—these will ever be a theme of just and unstinted praise. But the gods are jealous, and amidst such lavish endowments, they withheld from him a sympathetic imagination, without which no man can ever understand an alien people ; and it is a sad truth that to the end of his administration Lord Curzon did not really understand the people of India. This was at the root of his many inconsistencies and made him a perpetual puzzle to most men. . . . . Taking Lord Curzon at his highest, we find him engaged in a Herculean attempt to strengthen the Englishman's monopoly of power in India and stem the tide of popular agitation and discontent by rousing the members of the bureaucracy to a sense of duty similar to his own and raising the standard of administrative ability all round. The attempt has failed, as it was bound to fail. Never was discontent in India more acute and wide-spread than when the late Viceroy laid down the reins of office ; and as regards the beauracratic monopoly of power, I think we are sensibly nearer the time when it will be successfully assailed."*

Though the beginning of Lord Curzon's administration synchronised with a period of severe famines and acute distress, the twentieth century opened a new era in the eventful history of Indian finance. "The two years 1896-97 and 1897-98 showed a total deficit of 7 crores, but every subsequent year, including the two years of famine, yielded a considerable surplus. It was not necessary to impose fresh taxation ; and the only important fiscal changes made during the period were the reduction of the duties on cotton cloth from 5 to 3½ per cent. ; the exemption of cotton twist and yarn, and the imposition of a countervailing duty to protect Indian refined sugar against the competition of bounty-fed best sugar imported from Europe.

* Presidential Address at the Benares Congress, 1915.

From 1897-98 onwards the revenues have mounted up year by year, and the gross revenue of 1901-02, which showed a surplus of nearly 8 crores, exceeded by more than 16 crores the gross revenue of the prosperous year 1895-96."* The first few years of the twentieth century were years of recurring surpluses and the *regime* of Lord Curzon was one of extraordinary activity. His 'twelve tasks' have now become famous and commissions and inquiries were the order of the day. There was no department of Government which did not receive the Viceroy's attention and there was no aspect of the life of the country which escaped his scrutinising eye. Foreign policy, currency, education, famines, land revenue, irrigation, police, railways, co-operation and what not were questions examined by the indefatigable Viceroy and there was more movement and activity all round than during any other administration. The year 1899-1900 had closed with a surplus of more than 4 crores of rupees, and the next year was calculated to show an excess of about 2½ crores of revenue over expenditure. Sir Edward Law expected the year 1901-02 to yield a surplus of a little more than 1 crore. In his Financial statement, the Finance Member laid down the following proposition :—" In my opinion the question of economic development is one in which those responsible for the financial situation must take the keenest interest. It has always appeared to me that it is comparatively easy for a Government to

* Imperial. Gazetteer Vol. IV.

take money out of the pockets of the public, provided that those pockets are sufficiently well-filled. Hence I think we are specially interested in doing all that is in our power to promote economic progress." Sir Edward then proceeded to show how India was steadily growing more prosperous and to observe that 'the fact that we have been able to meet the extraordinary demands on our resources, due to famine and plague, and that we are to-day able to present a budget showing, notwithstanding the simultaneous serious depression in. three such important industries as cotton, tea and indigo, a distinct and satisfactory increase of revenue obtained without increase of taxation, is in itself the strongest evidence of that recuperative power.'

Here it is necessary to say a word with regard to the counter-vailing import duties on bounty-fed sugar. One of the earliest measures of Lord Curzon's administration was the imposition of these additional duties on sugar coming from countries the Governments of which granted bounties to exporters of sugar in order to stimulate the development of its manufacture. Beet-root sugar was manufactured in Germany and Austria-Hungary and exported in large quantities to India which was at one time the home of the sugar industry. The Viceroy felt that the competition which manufacturers of sugar in India had to face was extremely unfair and that it ought not to be allowed to kill the indigenous industry. It was contended on the other side that the nations which paid the bounty on the export of sugar, taxed themselves to that extent in order to supply India with cheap sugar, and that it would not be wise to discourage the imports of such a bounty-fed article by levying upon them a duty sufficient to counteract the effects of the bounty. In examining the effect of the extra duty, Sir Edward Law called attention, in his Financial Statement*, to the fact that the United Kingdom and the interested British Colonies, the Straits Settlements, Hongkong and Mauritius appeared to have had their full proportion of the share in the remarkable increase of importation into India, during the expiring financial year, and remarked that about 18 lakhs of rupees had been added to the revenues of India, the addition being realised at the expense of the European tax-payers taxed by their respective Governments to provide the bounties which enable foreign sugar-refiners to sell their sugar in India at prices below prime cost. Lord Curzon had not been deterred by the 'mutterings of the priests at the shrine of free trade' from imposing the extra duties and they were welcomed in India as a measure of protection to the indigenous industry of sugar manufacture. It was, however, pointed out at the time that though the Indian exchequer might gain a few lakhs more, the consumer in this country could not have any other compensation for the higher price he had to pay for his sugar than the consolation that the nations paying bounties mere punished and that their rivals were given an opportunity to drive them from the

* For 1901-1902.

Indian market. The Indian sugar industry got no direct stimulus or assistance and it was immaterial to it whether the competition came from Mauritius or from any other country. Herein lay the weakness of the case for the countervaling duties and the Hon'ble Mr. P. Ananda Charlu observed in the course of his remarks on the Financial statement for 1901-1902 as follows:—"The main ground on which the Act was sought to be passed and on which it was widely supported was that it would safeguard and promote the interests of the many thousands who had many thousands of acres under sugar-cane cultivation...It is unfortunate that the avowed intention is presumably unfulfilled, and that the suspicion freely expressed at the time, that it was legislation for the benefit of some of the colonies, seems not to have been altogether unfounded." There is always the danger of protective measures taken presumably in the interests of the people of India proving, in the end, beneficial to everybody except themselves. Our imports of foreign sugar have steadily advanced during the past many years and the indigenous industry has not made any appreciable progress during all this time.

II. A new era in the History of Finance.

The early years of the present century we have characterised as a new era in the history of Indian finance. It was an era of surpluses. Though the danger of famine and scarcity was ever present to the mind of Government, and increased military expenditure was not an unlikely possibility, one of the most disturbing factors in the financial situation had been entirely removed by this time, we mean the uncertainty of foreign exchange. Not only was the gold value of the token rupee permanently fixed by law at 16 d. and the possibility of a substantial fall in exchange precluded, but a very large saving was effected in the remittances to pay the Home charges. Taxation in India had been raised to a high level to enable Government to meet the increase in these charges caused by the falling exchange and that level was maintained even when the value of the rupee was artificially raised. Indian finances thus appeared to be extemely prosperous and even famines and pests seemed powerless to affect the situation adversely. We therefore notice a tone of optimism in the financial statements and official utterances which was not justified by the true character of the apparent prosperity of the country. The public treasury continued to overflow with surpluses year after year and it was felt that everything was for the best in this best of all lands. Those who spoke of India's poverty were put down as unreasoning and blind pessimists and the continued surpluses encouraged the spending proclivities of different departments. Few realised the true causes of the recurring surpluses. The masterful personality and fervid eloquence of the Viceroy carried everything before them. It was in a Legislative Council dominated by such a Viceroy as Lord Curzon that Mr. Gokhale had to fill the *role* of a fearless and well-informed critic of Government and to occupy the place vacated by Mr. Phrozesha Mehta. How he soon made a mark for himself, and fulfilled all the expectations of his friends and became himself a dominant figure in the Viceregal Council, will be clear from the sequel.

The revised estimate for the year 1901-02 showed a surplus greater than that anticipated in the original estimates by no less an amount than £3,982,000, about 6 crores of rupees, and the next year was calculated to yield a surplus of about 1¼ crore of rupees. And the Finance Member stated:—'The realisation of so large a surplus cannot but be a matter of congratulation to India, and, following the relatively large surplus which we were able to announce last year, it confirms the hope I then ventured to express, that, if no new ill-fortune overtakes us, we might, as regards finance, look forward to a period of increasing prosperity'. He pointed to certain considerations which, he thought, indubitably indicated the growing prosperity of the people though he depreached exaggerated optimism in view of a sudden turn the good fortune of the country might take at any moment. Mr. Gokhale's maiden speech in the Viceroy's Council on the Financial Statement for 1902-03, must have come as an unpleasant surprise upon the Government when they were congratulating themselves and others upon the continued and substantial prosperity of India, though his views upon this and cognate subjects were, by this time, well-known. Mr. Gokhale opened his budget speech with the following characteristic sentences :—" Your Excellency, I fear I cannot conscientiously join in the congratulations which have been offered to the Hon'ble Finance Member on the huge surpluses which the revised estimates show for last year. A surplus of seven crores of rupees is perfectly unprecedented in the history of Indian finance, and coming as it does on the top of a series of similar surpluses realized when the country has been admittedly passing through very trying times, it illustrates to my mind in a painfully clear manner the utter absence of a due correspondence between the condition of the people and the condition of the finances of the country. Indeed, my Lord, the more I think about this matter the more I feel—and I trust your Lordship will pardon me for speaking somewhat bluntly—that these surpluses constitute a double wrong to the community. They are wrong in the first instance in that they exist at all—that Government should take so much more from the people than is needed in times of serious depression and suffering; and they are also wrong because they lend themselves to every mis-interpretation and, among other things, render possible the phenomenal optimism of the Secretary of State for India, who seems to imagine that all is for the best in this best of lands."

III. The Phenomenon of Surpluses.

The large surpluses which accrued in the treasury from year to year were so striking that

* Financial Statement for 1902-03.

they could not be accounted for on the theory of the steady growth of prosperity in India. It was a comfortable theory no doubt but it ought to have failed to satisfy any discerning inquirer. The question was, how could there be continued surpluses in the national accounts when there was no sudden accession of wealth to the people and addition to the resources of Government? Superficial minds found an adequate explanation in the steadily improving economic condition of the people and they never paused to inquire whether that cause was sufficient to pour unexpected crores into the treasury. Mr. Gokhale saw at a glance the true character of the surpluses, and during the next few years continued to expose the fallacy which attributed them to the growing prosperity of the people. Thus was shattered the picture, which had been painted in glowing colours, of the taxpayer producing a steadily increasing quantity of wealth, securing a larger share of the national dividend and contributing a more substantial quota to the revenues of the State. The surpluses really meant something else. They meant that Government was taking more out of the pockets of the people than it was justified in doing and that more money was available to it than could be usefully spent on measures calculated to provide for the material and moral well-being of the mass of people. The secret of the surpluses was that they were 'mainly, almost entirely, currency surpluses, resulting from the fact that Government still maintained the same high level of taxation which they considered to be necessary to secure financial equilibrium when the rupee stood at its lowest.' It was in 1894-95 that the rupee touched this lowest exchange value, the average rate of exchange realised in that year being only 13.1 d. to the rupee. But the Government resolutely maintained an equilibrium between their revenue and expenditure by large and continuous additions to the taxation of the country and even in the year 1894-95, the national account sheet showed a surplus of 70 lakhs of rupees. From this time onward, owing to the operation of the currency measures taken by Government in 1893, the exchange value of the rupee rose steadily, and except during the two famine years 1896-97 and 1897-98, which showed deficits of 1·7 crores and 5·38 crores respectively, there accrued in the national accounts substantial surpluses from year to year. This movement corresponded exactly to the upward movement of the exchange which established itself in the neighbourhood of 16 d. per rupee in 1898-99. A rise in exchange meant a saving to the Government of India in the amount of Home charges which had to be provided every year. A difference of one penny per rupee meant a difference of about one crore of rupees in that amount. And the fact that the exchange value of the rupee had risen from 13 d. to 16 d. was sufficient by itself to explain the large surpluses of the four or five years that succeeded the famine of

1897-98. The following table compiled by Mr. Gokhale is very instructive in this connection :—

Year.	Deficit or Surplus in Crores of Rs.	Extra-ordinary charges for war and Famine relief.	Total surplus but for the extra charges.	Remarks.
1897-98	— 5·36	9·21	3·85	A year of famine and war.
1898-99	+ 3·96	1·09	5·05	Frontier operations.
1899-1900	+ 4·16	3· 5	7·66	A year of famine.
1900-01	+ 2· 5	6·35	8·85	Ditto.
1901-02	+ 7	1·	8	
Total for 5 years.	12·26	21·15	33·41	

Had there been no extra charges for war and famine, the revenues would have exceeded the expenditure by about 6¾ crores a year. Even making allowance for unexpected increases in revenue and reductions in expenditure, we may still put down the average surplus at 5 crores per year, which was also the figure of the amount saved by Government on their Home Charges as a consequence of the rise in the value of the rupee from 13 d. to 16 d. Government went on meeting every year's expenditure by that year's revenue and securing equilibrium by additional taxation. The result of this policy was to fix the taxation of the country at a level far above the actual needs of the situation. In India people have no control over taxation and no constitutional voice in shaping the national policy. 'If we had any votes to give, and the Government of the country had been carried on, by an alternation of power between two parties, remarked Mr. Gokhale, 'both alike anxious to conciliate us and bid for our support the Hon'ble member would assuredly have told a different tale.'

Mr. Gokhale expressed surprise that the Finance Member should have budgeted for a small surplus of 1¼ crores only when three times the amount would have been nearer the mark, particularly in view of the fact that four continuous years of fat surpluses had preceded and there was no dark cloud threatening the horizon. There was absolutely no justification for maintaining taxation at a high level, and the obligation to remit taxation in years of assured surpluses went with the right to demand additional revenues from the people in times of financial embarrassment. If he had not framed his budget in an exceedingly cautious manner, bordering on timidity, the Finance Member would have been able, for instance, (1) to take off the additional 8 annas of salt duty, (2) to raise the taxable minimum of the income-tax to at least Rs. 1,000 a year, and (3) to abolish the excise duty on cotton goods and yet to show a substantial surplus for the year 1902-03. A succession of large surpluses, Mr. Gokhale maintained, is little conducive to economy and is apt to demoralise even the most conscientious Governments by the temptations it offers for indulging in extravagant expenditure. In a country like India where public revenues are administered under no sense of responsibility, such as exists in the West to the governed, he would lay down the following governing principle of finance. 'A severe economy and vigorous retrenchment of expenditure in all branches of the Administration, consistently, of course, with the maintenance of a proper standard of efficiency, ought always to be the most leading feature—the true governing principle—of Indian finance, the object being to keep the level of public taxation as low as possible, so as to leave the springs of national industry free play and room for unhampered movement.' And he referred to two root-facts which must be borne in mind in considering the level of taxation in India and the administration of the revenues raised viz. (1) that it is the finance of a country a considerable part of whose revenue is by reason of its political and military necessities, spent outside its borders and *ipso facto* brings no commercial equivalent to the country and (2) that it is the finance of a country which is not only 'poor, very poor,' as Lord George Hamilton admitted, but the bulk of whose population is daily growing poorer under the play of the economic forces which have been brought into existence by British rule.

Before the Council reforms of 1909, the budget debate was the only opportunity which members of our legislative bodies could get to discuss various questions of financial, economic and administrative importance and they aired their views at the time on all manner of topics. Mr. Gokhale's budget speech of 1902 was a masterly exposition of the financial and economic situation in India. He showed a rare grip of principles and facts and he presented his case for reform in such an able manner that he was at once accounted as a formidable critic of Government. In his first budget speech in the Viceregal Council, besides the phenomenal surpluses, Mr. Gokhale offered very weighty remarks on the economic condition of the masses which Sir Edward Law had sought to prove in his financial statement, as satisfactory, on military expenditure, on land revenue policy and a variety of other subjects. The speech was a closely reasoned utterance full of vigour and earnestness—characteristics which were seldom absent from his addresses and it cannot but have made a profound impression upon the official world. It was highly admired for its tone of independence, for its insight into the principles of finance and for the intimate acquaintance with facts which it evinced. The Finance Member's reply was utterly feeble and Mr. Gokhale further developed and emphasised his views in the next year's budget speech. We shall see, as we proceed, how he never lost sight of the fundamental principles of policy he wished to enforce and returned to them, time after time, with the desire to win recognition for them and to get them adopted in actual practice. One of these cardinal principles was that the level of taxation should not be higher than was absolutely necessary, and if there were surpluses, they should be spent on urgent reforms calculated to promote the material and moral well-being of the people, or they should be returned to the people by remission of taxation.

IV. Remission of Taxation.

The criticism Mr. Gokhale had passed upon the large recurring surpluses and the unjustifiably cautious manner in which the budgets were framed, hit its mark. Every word appeared to have told, and in his financial statement for 1903-04, Sir Edward Law referred to the need of his estimates approximating more closely to the actuals but accounted for the divergence between the two by pointing to the uncertainty of agricultural conditions in India, which determined the whole financial situation. The surpluses of the four previous years, he admitted, had been obtained in spite of the fact that the period under review commenced with a terrible famine but he thought they afforded 'the strongest evidence of the recuperative power of the country and of the efficiency of the measures which have been taken by the Government in years past for its development.' Sir Edward would not accept Mr. Gokhale's explanation of the surpluses viz. that they were due to the rise in the value of the rupee and the consequent saving which Government made upon their Home Charges. The results of the closing financial year, he said, had been such as to confirm Government's confidence in the future and that it was their special good fortune to be able to announce that they felt themselves justified for the first time since 1882 in deciding on important measures in the direction of remission of taxation. It was freely admitted that in view of the existing satisfactory situation it was neither desirable, nor good financial policy, to continue levying taxation at rates yielding such large recurring surpluses as had been realised during the past few years. In his budget speech Mr. Gokhale gave expression to his feeling of sincere pleasure that the Finance Member had at last been able to advise Government that the time had come when the claims of the tax-payers, who had had to submit to continuous and ceaseless additions to the taxation of the country during the past 18 years, to some measure of relief might be considered.

Out of the three suggestions Mr. Gokhale had made in connection with the remission of taxation two were adopted. The three suggestions were the reduction of the Salt duty, a raising of the taxable minimum limit of the income tax and the abolition of the cotton excise duties. With the object of affording the most direct relief in the most suitable manner to the population at large, Government decided to reduce the Salt Tax in India, exclusive of Burma, from Rs. 2-8 per maund to Rs. 2, and to exempt from Income Tax all incomes belew 1,000 rupees per annum. Government have ever clung to the cotton excise duties with an obstinacy which is accounted for only by the political influence of Lancashire in the British Parliament to which Liberals and Tories alike are susceptible. The Salt Tax did not, in the opinion of Government, press hardly on the mass of the people, the actual impost per head being trifling.

But it was paid in the main by those who could least afford to contribute anything and Government hoped that the remission of even a trifling burden might prove a boon to the poorest class of tax-payers. Sir Edward Law proceeded to observe that a reduction of that tax had a very special recommendation in that it would provide a reserve which could be immediately and rapidly made use of by once more increasing the rate should such exceptional misfortunes as war or disastrous famine suddenly create an abnormal strain upon the resources of Government. In conformity with his principle that all possible economy should be practised in the administration of India and the funds thus made available should be devoted to the promotion of the moral and material development of the people, Mr. Gokhale urged, in his budget speech of 1903, the urgency of a reduction in military expenditure. He showed how the existing army system was extremely costly and pleaded for a policy of greater trust in the people. He observed:— "The policy of placing the main reliance for purposes of defence on a standing army has now been discarded every where else, and at the present moment, India is about the only country in the civilized word where the people are debarred from the privileges of *citizen soldiership* and from all voluntary participation in the responsibilities of national defence." Had the suggestion been received with favour as it deserved to be, India could have placed at the disposal of the Crown a larger army in the War with Germany and she could have been of greater material assistance to the Empire in the hour of need. "What I am anxious to see," observed Mr. Gokhale, "is the adoption of some plan whereby, while a position of greater self-respect is assigned to us in the work of national defence, the establishments necessary during peace and war times may be separated and thus our finances may be freed from the intolerable pressure of an excessive and ever-growing military expenditure."

V. Economic Condition of the People.

It was the practice of Sir Edward Law, in his Financial Statement, each year, to take a review of the general economic condition of the people and from commercial, revenue, banking and other statistics to demonstrate the steady progress the country was making. In his speech concluding the budget debate in the Supreme Legislative Council in 1901, Lord Curzon tried to give statistical proof of the growing prosperity of the country by pointing out that the average income per head of the population had risen from Rs. 27 in 1880 to Rs. 30 at the close of the nineteenth century. He returned to the subject again and again, and in 1902 did not feel that the financial situation justified any remission of taxation. Mr. Gokhale controverted the position the Finance Member had taken up in judging of the economic condition of the people from the proceeds of certain taxes and other supposed indications of prosperity. Disposing of other tests as fallacious, he had maintained that the only taxes whose proceeds supplied any indication of the material condition of the people, were the income tax and the salt tax—the former, roughly speaking, for the middle and upper classes and the latter for the masses, and held that the revenue under both these heads had been more or less stationary for years and the salt revenue had not even kept pace with the normal growth of the population. He therefore compiled tables from official publications and sought to establish the following propositions :—

(1) that the growth of population in the last decade has been much less than what it should have been and that in some provinces there has been an actual decline in the population ;

(2) that the death-rate per *mille* has been steadily rising since 1884, which points to a steadily increasing number of the people being under-fed ;

(3) that the consumption of salt, which already in this country is below the standard required for healthy existence, has not kept pace with even this meagre growth of population ;

(4) that the last decade has been a period of severe agricultural depression all over India ;

(5) that the net cropped area is diminishing in the older Provinces ;

(6) that the area under superior crops is showing a regrettable diminution ;

(7) the export and import figures tell the same tale, viz., that the cultivation of superior crops is diminishing. Cattle are perishing in large numbers.

In the opinion of Mr. Gokhale, these and similar facts, taken cumulatively, led to the irresistible conclusion that the material condition of the mass of the people in India was steadily deteriorating and to him the phenomenon was the saddest in the whole range of the economic history of the world. An inquiry into the condition of a few typical villages had been often suggested to Government and he repeated the request in vain. In his Financial Statement for 1903-04, Sir Edward Law again reviewed the economic situation and proved to his own satisfaction that it was steadily and surely improving. Mr. Gokhale remarked in his budget speech of 1903 that he was amazed at the Finance Member's idea of what he called the 'good progress' of the material prosperity of the people.

On the question of the economic condition of the people, there was a continuous duel between Sir Edward Law and Mr. Gokhale, each pointing out the faulty figures and fallacious reasoning of the other. The former relied upon statistics of increased revenue from salt, stamps, excise, customs and Post Office as a sure indication of growing prosperity. The latter picked holes in the figures and the conclusions, and Sir Edward remarked in his reply to the criticism of his budget :—" If criticisms are based on fallacious assumptions I am grareful for the opportunity of exposing fallacies. If they are well founded, I am still more grateful for being corrected." Lord Curzon was of opinion that judged by any or all of the tests that are commonly and fairly applied, taxation in India was neither excessive nor high, and the revenues of the country having produced continuous surpluses even after all the administrative needs had been met, Government thought the time had come for taking somewhat less from the people. The patience of the community had itself enhanced the case for remission and the total annual sacrifice of revenue accepted by Government amounted to 210 lakhs of rupees. This was an indirect but clear admission of the plea of Mr. Gokhale whom the Viceroy paid a well-deserved compliment by referring to his budget speech of 1903 as 'characterised by the great ability which we have learned to associate with his utterances.' The increase in the revenue from certain heads was satisfactory, so far as it went, but the phenomenal surpluses that continuously accrued in the national accounts could not be taken as an indication of growing prosperity. They were currency surpluses and represented the excess of revenue Government took from the people for many years to meet the losses caused by the low exchange and which it maintained long after the price of the rupee had been raised. This feature of the situation Government would not frankly accept and they had to explain away the surpluses in a round about and by no means convincing manner.

The fact of the poverty of India was undeniable and Lord Curzon did not deny it. He said :—" I do not wish it for a moment to be thought that, because we have been able to remit the best part of 1½ million sterling per annum in taxation, therefore there is no poverty in India. Far from it. There is enough, and far more than enough. The size and growth of the population, the character of their livelihood, and to some extent their own traditions and inclinations, render this inevitable. But I do not believe that the people are getting poorer. On the contrary, I hold that they are making slow but sure advances, and that in normal conditions, this progress is certain to continue." It is interesting to be told that India's poverty is inevitable on account of its size, and the character of the livelihood of the people as well as their traditions and inclinations. Mr. Gokhale expressed a sense of surprise and disappointment that a few palty increases in revenue under certain heads should be accepted by the Finance Minister of this country as conclusive evidence of our growing material prosperity when many most important indications pointed just the other way. He made a stirring appeal to Government to devote their energies to a vigorous and statesmanlike effort for the promotion of the material and moral interests of the people. The fallacy of regarding the increase in customs revenue as a sure sign of the material progress of the people he exposed by showing how the ever-increasing imports of foreign manufactured goods, far from indicating any increase in the country's purchasing power, connoted a corresponding displacement of the indigenous manufacturer. 'Thus, while the import of cotton goods has been for years past steadily increasing,' he said 'we know, as a matter of fact, that hundreds and hundreds of our poor weavers throughout the country have been and are being driven by a competition they cannot stand to give up their ancestral calling and be merged in the ranks of landless labourers.' This transformation of India from a country which had flourishing agricultural and manufacturing industries into a country preponderatingly agricultural and dependant upon imported manufactures, has long been going on and has been facilitated by the extension of railways. Mr. Gokhale's appeal to Government to turn over a new leaf in the book of economic progress, is so full of earnestness and statesmanship that we take the liberty of quoting his remarks on this subject at some length. He said :—

"My Lord, Indian finance seems now to be entering upon a new and mportant phase, and the time has come when Government should take advantage of the comparative freedom, which the country at present enjoys from the storm and stress of the past eighteen years to devote its main energies to a vigorous and statesmanlike effort for the promotion of the material and moral interests of the people. Speaking roughly the first half of the nineteenth century may be said to have been for

British rule a period of conquest and annexation and consolidation in this land. The second half has been devoted mainly to the work of bringing up the administrative machine to a high state of efficiency, and evolving generally the appliances of civilized Government according to Western standards. And I venture to hope that the commencement of the new century will be signalized by a great and comprehensive movement for the industrial and educational advancement of the people. After all, the question whether India's poverty is increasing or decreasing, under the operation of the influences called into existence by British rule—though of great importance in itself—is not nearly so important as the other question as to what measures can and must be taken to secure for this country those moral and material advantages which the Governments of more advanced countries think it their paramount duty to bring within the easy reach of their subjects. My Lord, I have no wish to judge, it is perhaps not quit. just to judge, the work done so far in these directions by the British Government in India by the standard of the splendid achievements of countries more fortunately circumstanced and having a more favoure able start than ourselves in the field. I admit the exceptional character of our Government and the conflicting nature of the different interests which it has got to weigh before taking any decisive action in this matter. But after so many years of settled Government and of unchallenged British supremacy, it is, I humbly submit, incumbent now upon the rulers of this country to gradually drop the exceptional character of this rule and conform year by year more and more to those advanced notions of the functions of the State which have found such wide, I had almost said, such universal acceptance throughout the Western world. European States, for years past, have been like a number of huge military camps lying by the side of one another. And yet in the case of those countries, the necessity of military preparedness has not come and does not come in the way of each Government doing its utmost in matters of popular education and of national industries and trade."

The urgent need of the moment was, therefore, a comprehensive scheme of mass education to be immediately taken in hand. The condition of education in this country was most deplorable and it was at the root of all our backwardness. While in

the West, the Governments of different countries were adopting, one after another, a system of compulsory and even free primary education for their subjects, in India alone the Government was making a paltry contribution to the education of the people though the Supreme Government had just adopted the policy of making special grants to education. Mr. Gokhale urged the necessity of making Education an Imperial charge so that the same attention which was bestowed by the Supreme Government on matters connected with the Army Services and Railway expansion, might also be bestowed on the education of the people. He quoted comparative figures of the funds devoted to education in India and other countries and concluded:—
"My Lord, even allowing for the difference in the purchasing power of money, in this country, and elsewhere, these figures tell a most melancholy tale and show how hopelessly behind every other civilized nation on the face of the earth we are in the matter of the public education." Here he laid down the sound principle that whenever there was a surplus, it should be appropriated to the work of promoting the educational and industrial interests of the country. Finance Members differed radically from Mr. Gokhale on this question. While they devoted surpluses, which only meant an excess of revenue taken from the people over the necessary expenditure of the year, to the reduction of the national debt, he wanted them to spend the surpluses in pushing on educational and industrial

progress. The public debt of India was comparatively small and there were valuable assets on the other side which covered the whole. It was therefore unfair that the surpluses should be devoted to the reduction of debt rather than directly spent on the promotion of the moral and material interests of the people. The intimate connection between financial policy and economic progress of the nation will thus be obvious. The question of the employment of Indians in the higher and more responsible offices in the administration is also closely connected with this problem. Under the existing system, the authorities to whom is entrusted the work of shaping the destinies of this nation, take a very limited view of their duties and are satisfied if the machine goes on smoothly. "The result is that there is an inveterate tendency to keep things merely going, as though every one said to himself, 'This will last *my* time.' What the situation really demands is that a large and comprehensive scheme for the moral and material well-being of the people should be chalked out with patient care and foresight, and then it should be firmly and steadily adhered to, and the progress made examined almost from year to year."

VI. The Surpluses Again.

The accounts for the year 1902-03 showed a surplus of 4½ crores, the revised estimates for 1903-04 put down the surplus at 4 crores and the financial statement for 1904-05 calculated upon an excess of revenue over expenditure of about one crore. The fact that such surpluses could be secured after the recent remission of taxation amounting to about two crores of rupees, was most striking. For 1904-05 the revenue was estimated at a little more than £ 80 millions and the expenditure at £ 79¼ millions. The figures for the three years may be thus presented :—

	Revenue.	Expenditure.	Surplus.
1902-3	£.	£.	£.
(Accounts)	77,434,915	74,365,366	3,069,549
1903-04			
(Revised Estimates)	83,067,800	80,356,600	2,711,200
1904-05			
(Budget Estimates)	80,148,600	79,229,900	918,700

The surplus of £ 2¾ millions for 1903-04 was in reality an amount reduced by special grants made to Provincial Governments and if they were included, the true surplus would have been £ 4 millions. The national accounts thus presented the extraordinary phenomenon of a year in which taxes bringing in a revenue of close upon two crores of rupees were remitted, showing, in spite of the remission, a surplus of about 6¾ crores. The question of the surpluses could not therefore but attract the serious attention of students of finance, and in his budget speech of 1904, Mr. Gokhale once more adverted to it. 'Never before, my Lord,' he said, 'were such huge surpluses realized in the history of Indian finance, and the fact that they have shown themselves year after year for six years in succession proves conclusively that the level of taxation has been fixed much higher than the needs of public expenditure require or the circumstances of the country justify.' He repeated his explanation of the phenomenon of surpluses and showed that the rise in the rupee and the recovery in the opium revenue had brought about an improvement of about eight crores a year in the financial position of the Government of India. If two crores remitted in 1903 were deducted and if it was assumed that the normal increases in the ordinary sources of revenue covered the normal increases in expenditure, the annual surplus came to about 6 crores a year. Mr Gokhale admitted that an equilibrium between the ordinary revenue and the ordinary expenditure was a necessity in a solvent nation's finance and that under unfavourable conditions, even extraordinary charges might be met out of revenue. To assure the position, a moderate surplus also must be provided for. But what was the actual position in India ? Year after year, more was taken from the pockets of the people than was necessary and it was but fair that those classes who had suffered from the high level of taxation should get relief when the strain on the resources of Government had been removed. Presenting the Indian Budget to Parliament, the Secretary of State had stated that the 'remission of taxation was mainly due to the success of our present currency policy'. Mr. Gokhale quite pertinently asked if the Secretary of State really imagined that such an impossible feat as that of raising the exchange value of the rupee without involving an indirect increase in the taxation of the country could be performed and inquired what was there to prevent us from still further increasing our surpluses by raising the rupee still higher—say to 1 s. 6 d. or even 2 s.? He therefore submitted that the authors of the currency policy should freely admit that whatever its counter-balancing advantages might be, that policy involved a most heavy indirect addition to the burdens, especially of the agricultural population when its full effects manifested themselves.

In his Financial Statement, Sir Edward Law had put in an elaborate defence of the cotton excise duties. This subject has been discussed threadbare and arguments in defence of the continuation of that impost have been most successfully refuted. One of those advanced by the Finance Member was the loss of 20¼ lakhs which the abolition of the duty would involve. In fact, it was a funny argument in view of the plethora of money which the Government had in the country's exchequer and with which it did not know what to do. Mr. Gokhale therefore urged that the excise duties should go and that another eight annas should be taken off the salt duty. Another measure of relief he proposed was a lowering of the land revenue demand, especially in the North-West Provinces, Bombay and Madras. 'Land revenue stood at 24·04 crores in 1890-91 and the budget figure for 1904-05 was 29·36 crores, which meant an increase of 22 per cent. in 14 years. The increase of land revenue was out of all proportion to the increase in cropped area. Mr. Gokhale made a very strong appeal in favour of a reduction in the land revenue demand in view of the fact that 'the raiyat in most parts is a poor, struggling cultivator, with his resources all but exhausted and himself more or less involved in debt'. The condition of the national exchequer was satisfactory and would easily allow f the much-needed relief being granted. One of the important questions to which the indefatigable Viceroy had directed his attention was the systems of land revenue assessment in the various Provinces of India. The policy of Government in this matter had been subjected to a searching examination and severe criticism, and Lord Curzon thought it necessary to publish a lengthy Resolution examining the whole question in detail and attempting a reply to the public criticism. The importance of the subject requires more than a passing reference to this controversy though we cannot deal with it here at any great length.

VII. The Land Revenue Problem.

One cannot expect to have in India a uniform system of land tenure. As the various parts of the country came under British rule, the method of assessing the revenue to be taken from landlords and cultivators, was fixed at different times and in different ways. The vicissitudes of fortune of the holders of land gave rise to various titles and claims and it took generations for the Government to fix them definitely. While in Bengal and in northern parts of Madras, the State recognized proprietors of land whose revenue was permanently fixed, in other parts of the country the demand of the State was to be revised periodically and the revenue was to be taken from the cultivator directly without the interposition of a middleman. At one time, the idea was widely entertained by high officials that the system of permanent settlement which was introduced by Lord Cornwallis into Bengal, might, with advantage, he extended to other parts of the country and that the State might deal there with a Jamindar as in northern India. There were others, however, who held that the permanent settlement was a mistake, which had lost to the State an increasing source of revenue and ought not to be repeated elsewhere. It was also urged that dealing direct with the cultivator, the State, in its capacity of landlord, would confer a boon upon him by preventing a large part of his produce from being intercepted by a middleman landlord. The various systems of land tenure and land revenue settlement were thus steadily evolved and definiteness and permanence have now been imparted to them. There is no question as to the right of proprietorship of the *Jamindars* in Bengal, Madras and elsewhere as it has been definitely recognized by Government. That right in the case of cultivators in *rayotwari* parts is equally indisputable; but advocates of State-landlordism often throw doubts upon it. As regards the settlement of land revenue, there are some who look upon the Bengal system as ideal and recommend its extension to other parts. At the other pole there are people who would reserve to the State the power to raise the revenue whenever it deems fit to do so with a view to sharing the unearned increment—the increasing value of the land, the increase being brought about by the general progress of the community. They point to the loss the State has sustained owing to the land revenue being perpetually fixed in Bengal. In this connection, a writer states:—"The shares of the Zemindars and of the Government in the rental were in the ratio of 1 : 9 at the time of the Permanent Settlement. As the Government revenue in 1793 was nearly 360 lakhs, this represented nine-tenths of the total rental, which was therefore 400 lakhs. Now, the present rental is about 1,600 lakhs, which is four times the rental at the time of the Permanent Settlement. The Government revenue being now fixed at say 400 lakhs, a sum of 1,200 lakhs is shared between the rayats, the tenure holders, Zemindars &c.*

Midway between the two stand those who want neither a permanent settlement nor a revision of settlements at short intervals. They would only eliminate from the temporary settlements all elements of uncertainty and inquisitorial inquiry. This principle inspired the despatch of Lord Ripon, of 17th October, 1882. "His object was to give the agriculturist an assurance of permanence and security, whilst not depriving the State of the

* The Permanent Settlement in Bengal.—S. C. Ray.

power of enhancement of the revenue on 'defined conditions' :......Men like Canning and Lawrence had held that the land revenue should be fixed for ever, leaving to the people of the country all future increase in the profits of agriculture. Other administrators had held that the State should claim an indefinite increase of revenue from the increasing profits from agriculture. Lord Ripon's masterly scheme met the views of both schools. He left the door open for a continuous increase of the land revenue with the increase of prices. At the same time, he offered to the cultivators what was virtually a Permanent Settlement of the land revenue as represented in produce."* Lord Ripon's principle was not definitely accepted though the Secretary of State laid down certain rules in connection with assessments. The question was once more raised at the close of the last century by a number of prominent retired Civil Servants who submitted a memorial to the Secretary of State for India offering five suggestions to make the rules of land administration definite and clear, and more hopeful to the Indian cultivators. They urged that (1) the land tax should not be revised in any Province within thirty years of the expiration of a former revision; (2) where the land revenue is paid by landlords, the Government demand should be limited universally to one-half of the actual rent or assets of the landlords; (3) where cultivators pay direct, the revenue demand should not exceed

* India in the Victorian Age—R. C. Dutt.

50 per cent. of the value of the net produce and should not ordinarily exceed one-fifth of the gross produce ; (4) when revision is made, the assessment should not be increased except in cases where the land has increased in value (i) in consequence of improvements in irrigation carried out at the expense of Government or (ii) on account of a rise in the value of produce based on the average prices of the thirty years next preceding such revison ; and (5) the rate of local cesses on the land tax should not exceed 10 per cent., the Bengal rate of 6¼ per cent. being a fair one.

Mr. Romesh Chandra Dutt, who took a very deep interest in the question of land revenue, examined the systems prevalent in the various Provinces and addressed, in the course of the year 1900, Letters to Lord Curzon, pointing out their serious drawbacks and suggesting remedies. He took up one Province after another, gave a brief history of its settlement and revenue administration and pleaded for appropriate reforms. The devastating famine of the closing year of the last century, riveted public attention upon the land tax, and reforms in the direction of a clearly-defined limitation of the State demand upon the cultivator appeared to be absolutely necessary. Non-official members of the Viceregal Council referred to this question prominently in the course of the budget debate in 1900. Mr. Pherozesha Mehta gave a very humorous description of the procedure of revision operations, observing 'that even sending delegates to the Indian

National Congress has been used as an argument for a revision of the settlement'. He went on to observe :—" In making these remarks I do not mean to advocate a permanent settlement like that in Bengal. But it is well worth considering whether the scheme recommended by the Government of India in the time of Lord Ripon, under which assessments would be revised only in the case of a general rise of prices or of improvements made by the State at its own cost, does not deal with the question in a more reasonable and scientific manner. Under such a scheme the 'unearned increment' would be saved to the State, but it would be automatically measured by the rise in prices which would include all the sources of its growth." When the memorial was forwarded by the Secretary of State for India to Lord Curzon's Government, the Viceroy took up the question personally, as was his wont in all cases where grave matters of policy were involved. Instead of ordering an independent inquiry, however, he asked the opinions of the Local Governments who felt they had been put upon their defence. They therefore replied, justifying existing arrangements which were represented as superior to any that might be substituted. Lord Curzon summarised these views in a Government Resolution * which was published as a reply to the memorialists, who were told that the prevalent systems worked very well, on the whole, were suited to the peculiar conditions

* Resolution of the Governor General-in-Council, dated January 16, 1902.

of the several Provinces and could not be modified without inconvenience and detriment both to the cultivators and the Government. We cannot here go into the arguments of the Resolution against the adoption of the proposal, made by the memorialists, but would indicate the position of the rayats in Bombay and Madras, under the present system, in the words of Mr. Dutt. "It is a lamentable truth that the present proprietors of Madras and Bombay, paying the Land Tax direct to the State, have, at the present day, less security than the tenants of private landlords in Bengal. The Bengal tenant pays 11 per cent. of his produce to his landlord; the Gujarat rayat pays 20 per cent. to the State. The Bengal tenant knows the specific grounds on which his landlord can claim enhancement; the Madras and Bombay rayat does not know the grounds on which the State will claim enhancement at the next settlement. The Bengal tenant reckons beforehand the limits of his landlord's claims; the Bombay and Madras rayat cannot guess what the Settlement Officer's claims will be. The Bengal tenant can appeal to courts against excessive demands; the Bombay and Madras rayat can appeal to no Land Courts and no independent tribunal against unduly severe assessments. Certainty and definiteness in the rental make the Bengal tenant value his tenant right and enable him to free himself from the thraldom of the money lender; uncertainty and indefiniteness in the State demand make the Madras and Bombay rayat till his land without hope, without heart, without motive to save, and year by year, he is sinking deeper in indebtedness. The Marquis of Ripon proposed to bestow on the peasant proprietor something of the security which the Bengal tenant enjoys, but the proposal was negatived by the Secretary of State in 1885. Friends of the voiceless cultivators of India again appealed for such security in the closing days of the century; the appeal was rejected by Lord Curzon in January 1902."*

It was on behalf of these rayats that Mr. Gokhale pleaded when he urged that relief might be given to the poor cultivators by a reduction in the State demand of land revenue. He acknowledged with gratitude the reduction of assessment made by the Government of Bombay in the Gujarat districts, but observed that nothing had been done to give relief to the agriculturist of the Deccan whose condition had deteriorated to an alarming extent. Sir Edward Law appears to have been considerably nettled by his criticism and tried to prove that the condition of the agricultural masses was by no means as black as it had been painted. He burst out into the following remarks :—" The Hon'ble Mr. Gokhale is one of the multitude who stand at the door of the treasury and cry 'give ! give !' But not only does he desire increased expenditure, he is most anxious to abolish such taxes as already exist and with which present needs are met. We are not in a position to-day adequately to provide for expenditure on many and various worthy objects and particularly on education

* India in the Victorian Age.

in which he is keenly interested, and yet......with numerous unsatisfied demands for expenditure, the Hon'ble Member questions our whole fiscal policy and suggests that one of our most important resources, the land revenue or rent paid for lands, the property of the State, should be sacrificed." It is worthy of notice that Sir Edward claims land as the 'property of the State' and is unwilling to reduce the 'rent' paid for it by the cultivators who, according to him, would be mere 'tenants'. He then went on to correct Mr. Gokhale's calculations with respect to the increase of land revenue and concluded that 'the total revenue derived from land in 1890-91 was Rs. 19,71,14,000, and that for 1904-05, was estimated at Rs. 22,35,24,000, which meant an increase of 14.3 per cent. and not 22 per cent. as had been stated.

VIII. India's Balance of Trade.

In his financial statement for 1904-05, the Finance Member attempted to combat the view entertained by people that the excess of India's exports over imports represents a dead loss of wealth to the country and that 'India is paying for more than she receives under the three heads of imported goods, imported investment securities, and payment abroad of budgeted Government sterling charges.' This is again the drain theory, only stated in another form, and as we have dealt with the question at some length already,* it is not

* See page 41.

necessary to discuss it further than to indicate the nature of the remarks Mr. Gokhale made in connection with Sir Edward Law's statement. Students of Political Economy know how misleading are the usual statements about a country's 'balance of trade' and how 'balance of accounts' is the expression now used, the latter taking into calculation the 'invisible' imports and exports and thus assuring greater accuracy. There is a movement of wealth to and from a country which is not registered in the usual statistics and hence a serious error occurs in the calculation of the outgoings and in-comings. The political and economic position of India, in the nature of things, necessitates the export of a quantity of wealth for which a return is not obtained. It is well-known that the excess of Great Britain's imports over exports represents the profits which British shipping, banking and insurance enterprise brings into the country, besides the ordinary profits of manufacture. Similarly a portion of India's exports is the remittance of profits and savings made by European merchants, manufacturers, planters, and civil and military servants of the State. This is a plain economic fact which has to be acknowledged and every attempt to deny it or to explain it away must be futile. In his Review of the Trade of India for 1914-15, Mr. Findlay Shirras, Director of Statistics, observes :—"It was explained in the last year's trade review that there were many factors to be taken into consideration in determining the balance of trade of a country. The payments due to India are the value of the exports, the import of capital into India, and remittances from abroad to persons residing in India, including tourists, while the payments due by India are, besides the value of the imports, the Secretary of State's drawings, interest on capital invested in India through private channels, investments outside India of the earnings of merchants, lawyers, &c., residing in India, earnings of the steamer companies employed in the coasting and foreign trade of India, remittances to Indians residing in foreign countries, premiums and policies issued by the Insurance Companies outside India, &c." It will thus be seen that the balance of trade is a very complex affair, and that a portion of India's export represents profits of European merchants, manufactures, planters, officials &c. Dealing with the same question, Mr. Shirras says in another* place :—" It is well-known that in addition to the remittance to England of large sums on account of interest on capital invested in banks, Industries, mines and other enterprises, there are the home charges amounting approximately to Rs. 30 crores. If allowance be made for interest on money lent to Government and embarked in railways, banks and industries, for remittances of money by British subjects and foreigners resident in India, it is clear that at least Rs. 45 crores were remitted in 1913-14 for interest and services rendered ; in other words, a balance of exports over imports of over Rs. 21 crores indicates that some Rs. 24

* Review of the Trade of India in 1913-14, page 6, note.

crores of new foreign capital were probably at the disposal of India in the year under review." Let it be noted here that the excess of exports over imports including merchandise and treasure in 1913-14 was Rs. 21·37 crores, including Government transactions, and the difference between this sum and the amount of Rs. 45 crores which is normally due by India and must be remitted abroad annually, represents the new capital, as Mr. Shirras points out, which was at India's disposal during the year.

Having thus cleared the position let us return to Sir Edward Law's statement. His argument is briefly this: 'During the three years from 1900-01 to 1902-03, the excess value of exports over imports was £47·58 million sterling. From this total must be deducted £1·45 millions, being the value of rupee paper transferred to India during the period; while we must add to it a sum of £2·14 millions representing the value of the stores, arms, munitions and animals, supplied to the Home Government in connection with their requirements in South Africa and China. This gives us a net excess of exports in three years of £48·27 millions.' Sir Edward contended that this was also the amount of the Secretary of State's Council drawings during the three years, and thus the excess of India's exports over imports exactly balanced the amount of the Home Charges, and except for the Home Charges India did not pay for more than she imported. This line of argument of the Finance Member, Mr. Gokhale met by asking what became of the profits annually earned by English merchants in India, of the freight English companies earned, of the savings of English lawyers, English doctors, English civil and military servants of the Crown, and corrected Sir Edward Law's calculations by deducting from the total imports £16 millions, the amount of the capital raised annually in England and spent on Indian railways and irrigation works, for which there was no corresponding export and on the other side, from the Secretary of State's drawings the value of the stores for which provision was made in his current disbursements and which amounted to over £3 millions. This gave the sum of £18 millions which represented the amount India paid more than she received during the three years. This calculation did not include, it may be noted, the capital borrowed by private individuals or companies for minor industries. In reply the Finance Member, in his turn, sought to point out a flaw in Mr. Gokhale's figures, saying that the net borrowings of the Secretary of State amounted to about £9½ millions and the bulk of it was spent in India, only one-third of the borrowings for railways being devoted to the purchase of stores abroad, and the remaining amount being spent in India. This does not, however, appear to have strengthened his case, and his explanation about the profits of English merchants and savings of English lawyers and servants of the Crown &c., was far from adequate For instance, he stated that the English merchant remitted any important sums abroad only when he retired. But some merchants must retire from year to year; they do not retire all together, and therefore, every year, some amount must be remitted to England. If that is not so, why was an outcry raised against a falling exchange? Was it not because large sums had to be remitted abroad by Europeans in India, official and non-official? We need not, however, labour the point, and the correct view of the balance of trade in India is the one we have indicated above.

IX. Quasi Permanent Provincial Settlements.

In Section IV of Chapter II we have given * a brief account of the development of the system of Provincial Finance inaugurated by Lord Mayo, and drawn pointed attention to its defects and to proposed reforms. That system, modified in 1877 and but slightly changed in 1882 and at later revisions of the provincial contracts, continued till 1904, when an important step was taken with a view to the remedying of the evils which seriously marred the arrangements. It was felt (1) that the periodical revisions interfered with the continuity of provincial finance and that each revision involved a protracted and sometimes controversial discussion with the Local Governments. (2) Another evil complained of was the extravagance the system encouraged. It was described as a system of five-year budgets and Provincial Governments had little motive for economy or carefully matured plans of expenditure. (3) And lastly, the apportionment of the revenue to the

* See Pages 66 to 75.

several provinces was never made on any definite or logical principle. To remove these defects, and in particular to introduce an element of relative permanence into the settlements, the following arrangement was made: "Firstly, it has been decided to give the Local Governments a permanent, instead of a merely temporary interest in the revenue and expenditure under their control. Secondly, the assignments to the Local Governments will include a slightly smaller share of growing revenues. Thirdly, this share has been calculated so that each province separately, and all the provinces taken together, shall be placed in possession of an amount of growing revenues which bears approximately the same proportion to the provincial expenditure as the Imperial share of growing revenues bears to Imperial expenditure."* With some small exceptions the actual heads of revenue, Imperial, provincial or divided, were left unchanged, but the provincial shares of the divided heads were altered in accordance with the principles stated above. It was found, in applying these principles to the actual figures, that the aggregate provincial expenditure represented rather less than one-fourth of the whole, while the Imperial expenditure, which included the Army and the Home Charges, was in excess of three-fourths. These proportions were taken as the basis of the division of revenue between Imperial and Provincial, but numerous adjustments were made mainly to allow larger assignments being made to more backward Provinces and to permit

* Financial Secretary's Memorandum, 1904-05, page 66.

provision being made for various administrative reforms and works of improvement.

Subject to these adjustments, it was decided to divide heads of revenue and the corresponding heads of expenditure as follows:—

(1) In Bengal, United Provinces, Bombay and Madras, three-fourths Imperial and one-fourth Provincial;

(2) In the Punjab and Burma, five-eighths Imperial and three-eighths Provincial;

(3) In the Central Provinces and Assam, half Imperial and half Provincial.

These settlements were permanent in the sense that they were not subject to revision at the end of fixed periods. The Government of India, as the final authority in India responsible for the finances and administration of the country, of course, reserved to itself the power to revise the settlement with any or all provinces at any time whenever necessity might demand it. The power was obviously to be exercised when the new arrangements became unfair to a Province, to the Government of India or to other Provinces, or if the Supreme Government was confronted with the alternatives of either levying additional taxation or of seeking assistance from the Provinces. The scheme placed the Local Governments in a favourable position at the start, and special grants were made to them for specific improvements. Lord Curzon stated that the new arrangements were the foundations of a financial

before it, the Government expressed the general opinion that India should continue to enjoy the power of dealing with foreign nations in the matter of tariffs according to her own situation and needs. The Government, so far as it could form an opinion, thought that India had little to gain from being involved in any fiscal scheme. But at the same time it wanted to possess the power of retaliation on foreign countries which penalised Indian exports.* It is difficult, in this place, to give anything like an adequate account of the several measures, bearing upon the economic condition of the different classes in the community, which Lord Curzon's Government undertook. Mr. Gokhale spoke as follows with reference to them :—"An administration, in many respects the most strenuous, as it undoubtedly has been the most eventful, of any that the country has known for many years past, has formulated these changes after a prolonged inquiry, and the country is waiting to see how they work in practice when they are introduced. The advance that has been made this year in the matter of Provincial finance, the undertaking of a comprehensive programme of irrigation works that is expected as a result of the Irrigation Commission's labours, an improved Police Service, increased expenditure on education in all its branches, the institution of State scholarships for industrial education abroad, the establishment of an Agricultural College at Pusa, the encouragement of Co-operative Credit Societies—

* See the Author's "Indian Industrial and Economic Problems."

these and other measures will require a large outlay of public money, if they are not to disappoint the expectations that have been formed of them in the public mind."

On the question of the economic condition of India, there has ever been a divergence of opinion between officials and non-officials. In sheer despair Lord Curzon asked, "Is it not time, therefore, that instead of repeating hypothetical figures and calculations, that have been exposed until exposure has become tedious, our critics should recognize the fact that India is, on the contrary exhibiting every mark of robust vitality and prosperity?", and in his opinion there were few even among the most advanced countries of the world, that would not welcome an economic position as sound as that India enjoyed. He compared critics of the Government, of the type of Mr. Gokhale to an "amiable eccentric" who always put up his umbrella and insisted that it was raining when the sun shone. The attitude of Indians who are not satisfied with the pace with which the country is progressing and want Government to adopt radical and comprehensive measures of reform, cannot be appreciated by officials who are content with little and make much of it. Thus Sir Edward Law referred to Mr. Gokhale's 'usual habit in exhausting the vocabulary of adjectives in describing in fanciful language the impoverishment of the country and the abject destitution of the raiyat population.' His description of Mr. Gokhale is too interesting to be omitted. Said Sir Edward :—"When he takes his

autonomy and sought to dispose of the charge of undue centralization frequently brought against the Supreme Government.

X. Lord Curzon's Measures.

Lord Curzon's administration was a period of feverish activity and the Viceroy turned his attention to almost every subject of administrative efficiency and State activity. Bringing to a close the budget debate on 20th March 1904, he observed in connection with economic development:—"Our recent Resolution on Agriculture sums up the practical steps that have been taken for the encouragement and improvement of agriculture and for the active prosecution of scientific research. We now have our Inspector-General of Agriculture with a staff of scientific experts, we have the new institution at Pusa springing into being, where research, the training of students and experimental farming will be simultaneously taken in hand, we have strengthened the Provincial Agricultural Departments, reorganized the Civil Veterinary Department, so as to undertake the investigation of cattle diseases and the improvement of breeds of cattle, and created a board of scientific advice to co-ordinate the work that is being done in these and all other branches of scientific research in India." One important measure of Lord Curzon's time was the passing of the Co-operative Credit Societies Act, Act X of 1904. The poverty and indebtedness of the cultivator in India was proverbial, and the possibility of improving the credit of the rural population by the establishment of a system of co-operative credit societies had been engaging the attention of Government for some time. The question had been taken up independently in some Provinces and in certain cases practical steps had also been taken. In 1901 a committee was appointed by the Government of India to consider the whole subject in the light of the experience already gained. It was felt that no real advance was possible without legislation which was undertaken with the object of providing special facilities for the establishment of credit societies, of conferring upon them special privileges so as to encourage their formation and assist their operation and of taking precautions against the improper utilization by speculators and capitalists of privileges not intended for them. From very small beginnings, the co-operative movement has now assumed considerable proportions and the law was modified a few years later to meet new requirements. Lord Curzon also created a new Department of the Government of India for Commerce and Industry and the appointment of a new Member of Council for those purposes.

Just after the close of the Boer War, the late Mr. Chamberlain started his campaign in favour of Tariff Reform and inter-imperial free trade. The Government of India was called upon to submit its views on the question. In its Despatch of 22nd October, 1903, it reviewed the whole trade situation of India and as no definite scheme had been placed

seat at this Council table he, unconsciously perhaps, adopts the rôle and demeanour of the habitual mourner, and his sad wails and lamentations at the delinquencies of Government are as piteous as long practice and training can make them; but I have reason to believe that outside these precincts the Hon'ble Member's words are sometimes in a lighter vein, and we may, therefore, perhaps hope that his jeremiads do not seriously indicate a feeling of such utter despair as they tend to produce in those to whom he addresses them. There is nothing more distressing than the mental attitude of the mourner who refuses to be comforted."

XI. Plethora of Revenues and Remission of Taxation.

In spite of these petulant remarks of the Finance Member, the Hon'ble Mr. Baker, who succeeded him, announced in the financial Statement for 1905-06, a reduction of taxation, necessitated by the surpluses with which the treasury was overflowing. The year 1904-05 was calculated to close with the large surplus of £3,485,000 and it was estimated that on the existing basis, for the next year too, the surplus would be equally large. It was, therefore, decided to make certain remissions of taxation and also to devote considerable sums of money to the improvement of various branches of the civil administration. A further reduction of As. 8 was effected in the salt tax, the rate of duty being fixed at Re. 1-8-0 per maund throughout India exclusive of Burma where it was already Re. 1.

This meant a loss of Rs. 183 lakhs in the year 1905-06. Secondly, the famine cesses which had been imposed in 1898, in the United Provinces, the Central Provinces and the Punjab at rates of about 2 per cent. on the land revenue as a part of the measures then being carried out for the creation of the famine insurance fund, were abolished and involved a loss of Rs. 22½ lakhs of annual revenue. Thirdly, 7 lakhs of revenue were sacrificed for the improvement of postal facilities. Provision was likewise made for increased recurring expenditure for the reform of the Police, the extension of primary education, the development of agricultural experiment, research and instruction, and lastly, for the improvement of the financial position of District and Local Boards throughout India. The cost of these 7 measures was calculated at £2,495,000 and was distributed as follows:—

		£
Remission of Taxation	...	1,371,000
Increase of Postal Facilities	...	47,000
Reforms of Civil Administration	...	1,077,000
Total	...	2,495,000

It was only natural that Mr. Gokhale should have offered to the Hon'ble Mr. Baker, his warm congratulations on the financial statement, characterised by a remarkable grasp of principle, mastery of detail and lucidity of exposition. He was particularly pleased with the reduction of the salt tax which had been so often urged in the interest of the mass of people with whom it was a necessary of life in India, and earnestly trusted that Government would take another opportunity to carry the relief still further in view of the established fact that the relief directly benefited the poorest classes of the community. The National Congress had urged at Bombay in 1904, the giving of assistance to Local Boards and Mr. Gokhale rejoiced to find that Government had responded to the appeal. He then went once more into the question of the surpluses realized by the Government of India, which amounted, during seven successive years, in all to about 32½ crores of rupees, not including the special grants made to Provincial Governments from time to time. Rs. 12½ crores were, besides, earned by Government as profits upon the coinage of rupees and went to constitute the Gold Standard Reserve Fund and about 16 crores more were spent out of revenue for famine relief and extraordinary military charges. This makes a total of about 49 crores, representing the excess amount taken by Government from the people in seven years over and above the requirements of the administration. The inevitable result of such plethora of money at the disposal of Government, was an increase in public expenditure, notably under Army services, on an unprecedented scale, though about 36½ crores had been devoted to the repayment or avoidance of debt. Such a system of finance, Mr. Gokhale submitted, was unsound in theory and indefensible in practice, for it involved a grievous injustice to the present generation. And he laid down a proposition of financial policy which ought to find acceptance at the hands of those who are responsible for the finances of this country. He said :—" In all countries, it is an accepted canon of finance that the weight of public burdens should be kept as light as possible and the scheme of taxation should be so fixed and adjusted as to meet, but no more than meet, public requirements under normal conditions. If this is so in rich European countries, it should be much more so in India, where the revenue is raised from a poor, helpless population, and the larger part is contributed by a broken and exhausted peasantry, and where, owing to the special circumstances of the case, the character of public expenditure is such that a great portion of it has to be spent on objects unconnected or but remotely connected with the moral and material advancement of the people."

XII. Growing Military Expenditure.

One of the biggest items of expenditure on which Mr. Gokhale spoke, year after year, was the ever-growing charge of the Army. That charge had doubled itself in twenty years, having risen from 17·9 crores in 1884-85 to 32·6 crores in 1905-06. The Indian Army was maintained at an extremely costly level, not for the simple purpose of the defence of India, but as 'a main factor in the maintenance of the balance of power in Asia.' The range of the military responsibilities of India in Asia had been enormously extended and their burden was thrown upon the shoulders of the poor tax-payers of this country. This new and Imperial definition of India's position and responsibilities was calculated, 'to stagger the people of this country' for it meant that India's resources were to be unhesitatingly used for engaging in a race with European Powers to absorb Asiatic Kingdoms. "The maintenance of the balance of power in Asia', said Mr. Gokhale, 'is a matter of Imperial concern; and for the Government of India to accept that responsibility is to impose upon this country a military duty and a military obligation to which she is utterly unequal and which, moreover, it is unjust to throw on her.' And yet, in view of the developments which were taking place in Asia, the Government of India decided, on the urgent advice of Lord Kitchener, the Commander-in-Chief, to carry out his scheme for the redistribution and reorganization of the Army at a cost of 15 crores. So far as the financial aspect of the scheme was concerned, having regard to its great magnitude and lasting character, Mr. Baker thought, we should have been justified, according to the practice of most other nations, in providing for it from loan funds; but the surpluses in the Indian exchequer were too tempting for the adoption of this principle and it was decided to make the necessary provision from current revenues. The total grants for Re-organization in 1905-06 were to amount to more than 3½ crores and Government proposed to allot a sum of 3 crores per annum for the prosecution of the scheme till it was completed. When the scheme was fully carried out, the Finance Member thought, it would involve a considerable permanent addition to Indian expenditure in the form of recurring charges.

No wonder, Mr. Gokhale protested most earnestly against this decision of the Government of India. It was most unjust to the people of this country to provide for the scheme of Army reorganization out of current revenues by yearly allotments and thus to keep up the high level of taxation for an indefinite period. The evil of large recurring surpluses was thus demonstrated to the hilt, and the helplessness of the people who have no constitutional power to control or influence the administration of their finances by Government, was seen at its worst. The Hon'ble Sir Edward Ellis had, in referring to Mr. Gokhale's criticism, the previous year, remarked on his ignorance of matters military and asked what would have been the fate of Japan in her war with Russia if her destinies had been guided by statesmen holding the views of the Indian critics of Government's military policy. Mr. Gokhale gave a spirited and dignified reply. He said:—"I do not think the reference to Japan was quite a tactful thing. For Japan's destinies are guided by her own sons, whose one thought and aspiration is the greater glory of their country, furthering by every means in their power the moral and material advancement of their people. Is the Hon'ble Member prepared to adopt Japan as a model for all branches of the country's administration? If so, let him induce his colleagues in the Government to treat the people of India as the Japanese Government treats the people of Japan in matters of education, of industrial development, of military and naval service, of appointment to high and responsible office, and I, on my part, humble as I am, undertake to see that no Indian publicist raises any objection to such military expenditure as the Hon'ble Member thinks it necessary to incur."

Two more questions dealt with in Mr. Gokhale's budget speech of 1905 were those connected with the reduction of land revenue in the temporarily settled districts and the appointment of Indians to high posts in the administration of their own country. He pointed out how the burden of taxes on land was heavy even according to official estimates, and how the agricultural classes were resourceless, and burdened with debt and urged that the fearful poverty and indebtedness of the cultivator called for a great and comprehensive scheme of ameliorative action. The second question had reference to the employment of Indians in the public service. It had engaged the attention of the Government and the public for several years and in spite of commissions, inquiries and Resolutions, the wishes of the people remained ungratified. Lord Curzon referred to that question in 1904 in his budget speech and the Government of India issued a Resolution in May of that year. In that Resolution the Government came to the astounding conclusion that not only were the people of this country not justified in complaining of exclusion from high office, but that they were being treated with 'a liberality unexampled in the history of the world.' It was not a difficult matter to expose the hollowness of the excuses which were put forward practically to exclude Indians from positions of trust and responsibility in their own country and Mr. Gokhale showed how inaccurate and misleading was the conclusion which the Government had recorded on the subject in their Resolution. The Viceroy expressed his warm sympathy with the aspirations of the Indian people but defended himself in his position of excluding Indians from higher posts behind the walls erected by the Public Service Commission of 1887. The question practically stands to-day where it did in Lord Curzon's time though we have had any number of discussions upon it and also another Commission to inquire into the legitimate complaints of the people.

CHAPTER IV.

PERSISTENT AND EFFECTIVE.

I. A New Regime.

The four years which succeeded the strenuous and fateful administration of Lord Curzon, constitute a period which has certain well-marked features. That period lies between two important epochs. The era of feverish administrative activity had closed and that of the reformed Legislative Councils was yet to come. The years when the Finance Member used to be overwhelmed with persistent surpluses were ended and the times of financial difficulties were coming. Lord Minto succeeded to a legacy of troubles left by his predecessor. The partition of Bengal had spread discontent throughout the land, the exotics of anarchy and sedition were taking root in places and repression seemed to be the only remedy to cope with the evil. Lord Morley had, however, become Secretary of State for India and gave rise to lively hopes in the breasts of educated people who anticipated great things from that liberal and liberty-loving philosopher. In the gloom which filled the country, the ray of expectations glimmered now and again. Lord Minto, the new Viceroy, proved a liberal-minded and sympathetic statesman, and he and Lord Morley, between them, evolved a scheme of Council reform, which, though it did not come up to popular demands, constituted a modest instalment of constitutional devèlopment. Mr. Gokhale played a very important part in the acquisition of the reforms, and his influence on the Government and the people was constantly on the increase. His advocacy o the cause of India's progress, in England and in this country, was vigorously continued and he had now established a reputation for earnestness of purpose sobriety of view, unerring insight into things and reliability of judgment. India was then passing through very difficult times. The general outlook was gloomy, new ideas had got hold of a section of the educated public and the ship of the Indian political movement was being tossed on the waves of a fearful storm. Mr. Gokhale was one of the few veterans who held the helm fast and guided the bark through rocks and shoals to a safe haven.

From the point of view of finance, India was entering on a new period. Large surpluses were a thing of the past. The last year of this period was a year of famine, and deficits made their appearance after a very long time. During all these years, Mr. Gokhale resolutely continued to press for reforms. He held firmly to his principles of sound finance, and his criticism of the budgets appeared to greater advantage on account of the experience of the past few years he brought to bear upon the discussion of financial and other questions. Of course, in certain important matters of policy, for instance, military expenditure and the employment of Indians in the public services, his persistent advocacy was not likely to bear much fruit. But there can be no doubt that his method of reiterating and enforcing his views, year after year, was most instructive and in many cases effective too. Several of his suggestions were accepted and acted upon by the Finance Member, and he never tried of putting forth proposals of economic reform. Mr. Gokhale never lost sight of the goal of his mission in the Viceroy's Council as outside it. He wanted his countrymen to become a stronger and a happier people and his nation to occupy a high status among the countries of the world. The spread of education, the improvement of sanitation, the promotion of indegenous industries and commerce, the relief of poverty, distress and indebtedness and the creation of a general tone of moral, intellectual and political elevation were the objects he strove to attain and his speeches in the Council and elsewhere were directed towards this end. This is the thread which runs through all his speeches, financial or otherwise, and it is this feature which lends so much interest and importance to all his utterances and activities. His gaze is steadily fixed on the goal and he never swerves or slips from the lines he has laid down. Any one reading his budget speeches will be struck with the reiteration of views with the sameness of the proposals and remedies and with the uniformity of the spirit of earnestness which animates his stirring appeals to Government. In this characteristic of his advocacy of reforms, however, lies, in our opinion, the main value and secret of Mr. Gokhale's work as a mission of progress.

The budget for 1906-07 anticipated a revenue of about £86½ millions and an expenditure slightly more than £85½ millions, leaving a surplus of a little more than £¾ million. The following comparative figures will be found interesting :—

	Revenue	Expenditure	Surplus.
	£	£	£
1904-05 (Accounts)	84,812,971	81,356,905	3,456,066
1905-06 (Revised Estimates)	84,829,500	83,073,800	1,755,700
1906-07 (Budget Estimates)	86,495,100	85,621,000	874,100

II. Cesses Remitted.

Had the expenditure in 1906-07 been left at the level of the preceding year, the Finance Member would have had a very large surplus at his disposal. He, therefore, wisely decided to devote the surplus to the carrying out of certain measures of administrative reform to the reduction of local taxation on the land and to the relief of certain local authorities at the expense of Imperial revenues. Mr. Gokhale expressed his sincere satisfaction at the policy underlying these measures and hoped that the salt tax would be still further reduced and brought down to Re. 1 per maund. There were many people who held that the burden imposed on the masses by a high salt duty was, after all, only slight and that the reduction of the rate could not seriously affect consumption. From the figures quoted by Mr. Baker it was clear that the reductions of the tax on salt, had increased the consumption of that article, and Mr. Gokhale laid down the incontestable proposition which he had so often put forward viz., that in dealing with a prime necessary of life, such as salt, the only right policy is to raise an expanding revenue on an expanding consumption under a diminishing scale of taxation. Twenty five lakhs per annum were given away out of the surplus for the reform of the Police, four lakhs per annum for agricultural development over and above the similar grant of 20 lakhs per annum made the previous year, a small sum of five lakhs a year for education, half of it being applied to technical education and the remainder to the education of Europeans and Eurasians.

The agricultural tax-payer next attracted the attention of the Finance Member, and he decided to give him relief on the lines followed in the previous year when certain famine cesses in Northern India and the Central Provinces were abolished. It was now proposed to abolish the cesses which were levied under various names such as the Patwari cess, the village service cess and the like, in Madras, the Central Provinces, the United Provinces and the Punjab. These cesses went to maintain village establishments and land records and were administered by Government and not by any local authority. With certain minor exceptions, they were all abolished and the Provincial Governments took over the entire liability for maintaining the above establishments, receiving compensation from Imperial revenues for the additional charges thus thrown upon them. It was the practice of the Provincial Governments to make certain petty appropriations from the funds of District and Local Boards for various provincial purposes, such as the district post, normal schools, &c. This was felt as a blot on the way in which local funds were administered, and now it was arranged to give the local bodies their revenues intact. The charges till then defrayed from the appropriations were to be paid by the Local Governments and the latter were to receive compensation from Imperial revenues. The policy underlying these arrangements was stated to be this: 'that no local cesses shall be imposed on the land, supplemental to the land revenue proper, except such as are levied by or on behalf of local authorities for expenditure by them on genuinely local objects; in other words, local taxation on the land shall, as far as possible, be limited to what is required for local administration by local bodies and shall not form an asset of Imperial and Provincial revenues.'* The Finance Member claimed that during the two years, 1905-06 and 1906-07, 'we shall have remitted or transferred to the local account items aggregating 110½ lakhs per annum' and that by these measures 'not only was substantial relief afforded to the taxpayers, but that most of the more important execrescences which have grown

* Financial Statement for 1906-07.

up around our system of local taxation have been cleared away.'

Before proceeding to deal with the larger question of economic reform, Mr. Gokhale made two suggestions and addressed one inquiry to the Finance Member. The first suggestion had reference to the manner in which receipts under the headings, Railways and Irrigation, were presented in the budget. The growth of receipts from these two heads taken by themselves signifies nothing and often times misled people. What was material was the net gain made by the State on these commercial undertakings and it was suggested that the true gain alone should be shown in the financial statement. Secondly, it was proposed that the income and expenditure of Local Boards, included under the head of Provincial Rates, should be separated from the account of the Government of India. The existing method was calculated to cause confusion. As to the inquiry, Mr. Gokhale wanted to know what was going to be done with the profits from coinage which were accumulating in the Gold Reserve Fund. The limit of £10 millions at first imposed, had been already passed and it was suggested that the profits might be used to provide money for loans to agriculturists in a comprehensive scheme for the relief of agricultural indebtedness. The justification of the policy of the State which invested its own money at 2½ per cent. and borrowed at the same time for its purposes at 3½, was not very clear. The Hon'ble Mr. Baker was in agreement with Mr. Gokhale with regard to the two suggestions and admitted their reasonableness. As to the limit of the Gold Standard Reserve Fund, he was of opinion that the figure mentioned by Sir Edward Law viz. 20 millions had not been reached and expressed his deliberate opinion that "every rupee that we coin from bullion may eventually have to be converted back into bullion and the profit which we made from the first operation must be religiously reserved to meet the cost of the second." Every penny of the profits from the coinage of rupees was linked with an equivalent liability which was none the less real because it might not have to be discharged for a long time to come. Sooner or later gold was bound to come into general circulation in India and Government would be called upon to dispose of the surplus stock of rupees and replace them by gold. Recent experience has confirmed the wisdom of having a large stock of gold in the Gold Reserve for the purpose of supporting exchange and in the opinion of experts, the highest limit of the Reserve is not yet in sight.

III. Growing Military Expenditure.

Even at the risk of tiresome repetition, we must emphasise the important fact that the problem of financial reform in India is intimately and vitally bound up with popular control over the administration of expenditure and the general policy affecting the government of the country. How revenues shall be raised and expended in India, must be determined solely in the interests of the people of this country and mainly by them too. The method of expenditure is regulated by the policy of Government and if the people have no effective share in the shaping of that policy, they cannot regulate the expenditure in accordance with what they consider to be their interests. The Government of India itself cannot determine this policy. And in his budget speech of 1906, Mr. Gokhale stated that 'a protest in this country against the military policy of Government and the ceaseless and alarming growth of our military burdens is almost like a cry in the wilderness.' He said, however, that the protest was to be made on every occasion that presents itself as India's most vital interests are involved in a proper solution of the question. Moreover, if there was a juncture when the voice of Indian public opinion required to be raised and heard by the authorities, that juncture was the close of the Russo-Japanese War. In this connection Mr. Gokhale made the following observations :—" A profound change has taken place in the general position of Asiatic politics. The triumph of Japan in the late war has ensured peace in Mid and East Asia. The tide of European aggression in China has been rolled back for good. The power of Russia has been broken; her prestige in Asia is gone ; she has on her hands troubles more than enough of her own to think of troubling others for years to come ; and thus a cloud that was thought to hang for twenty years and more over our North-Western Frontier has passed away, and, humanly speaking, is not likely to return, at any rate, during the time of the present generation. The Anglo-Japanese alliance concluded without considering how it would be regarded by the people of this country, is a further guarantee of peace in Asia, if such an alliance has any meaning. Surely My Lord, this is the time when the people of this country have a right to look for a substantial relief from the intolerable burden of our excessively heavy military expenditure which they have had to bear for so many years past." He therefore respectfully protested against the execution of the scheme of Army reorganization, as involving an expenditure of money and effort wholly beyond the capacity of the Indian tax-payers and neither called for nor justified by the requirements of the situation. If, however, it was decided to proceed with the scheme, Mr. Gokhale strongly urged that the money required for the initial outlay, should be found out of loan funds. He also suggested that the strength of the Army in India should be reduced by at least those additions that were made in 1885. The growth of military expenditure will be seen from the following figures :—

1884-85	...	17·9 crores (Before the increases of 1885 were made).
1888-89	...	22·2 crores (After the increases had their full effect).
1902-03	...	28·2 " "
1906-07 (Budget)		32·8 " "

It will be realised from these figures how enormous had been the increase in the military expenditure, which, in fact, overshadowed the whole field of Indian finance and under its chilling influence, no healthy development was possible. While the surpluses accruing in the treasury were being used as capital, increasing military expenditure was provided from revenue. The Imperial Government which was mainly interested in this increase and in the maintenance of the balance of power in Asia, made no contribution to this heavy expenditure. The principle on which the Finance Member acted in this connection, he reiterated in his speech of 1906, viz. that "it would not be sound or expedient to have recourse to borrowing for the purpose of carrying out the scheme of Army organization unless we should find it impossible to finance it without undue difficulty out of revenue." Both His Excellency the Commander-in-Chief and the Viceroy tried to reply to Mr. Gokhale's criticisms. Both of them pleaded that the Army expenditure was absolutely necessary for the efficient defence of the country and the latter argued that the assumptions of Mr. Gokhale with respect to the position of Russia and the general situation in Asia, were not justified. The question of the Army expenditure was not, however, only a question of finance. It was bound up with the demand of the people that the higher military careers should be thrown open to them and they should be trusted to take an important part in the defence of their own country and the Empire. Besides the growing military expenditure, another question at issue between Mr. Gokhale and Finance Members was the principle which should govern the utilization of surpluses.

The latter held the view that if a surplus accrues either from a fortunate windfall or from sources the continuance of which is not assured, it can not be used more advantageously than in the construction of remunerative public works, while the former urged that there were many extremely useful objects on which the surplus could be spent to the great benefit of the people. 'Are railways everything?' asked Mr. Gokhale, 'is mass education nothing, is improved sanitation nothing, that the Finance Minister should lay hands on every rupee that he can get either by borrowing or out of surpluses and devote it to the construction of Railways only?' The fact that the surpluses were uncertain was immaterial as they were to be spent only when they were available.

IV. The Right and the Wrong use of Surpluses.

The surpluses which had become a familiar feature of Indian budgets, were rendered possible, we need not repeat, by the artificial enhancement of the rupee and were realized by the maintenance of taxation at a higher level than was necessary, by a systematic under-estimating of revenue and over-estimating of expenditure. And they had the inevitable effect upon the expenditure of the country. With abundance of money in the exchequer, the level of expenditure was bound to be pushed up. 'Economy came to be a despised word and increased establishments and revised scales of pay and pension for the European officials became the order of the day.' The most pressing needs of the country in egard to the moral and material advancement of the people continued, for the most part, unattended to and no advantage of the favourable financial position was taken to inaugurate comprehensive schemes of State action for improving the condition of the masses. Mr. Gokhale stated that the three evils to be combated in connection with the raiyat's position were his (1) fearful poverty, (2) his ignorance and (3) his insanitary surroundings, and proceeded to indicate the lines on which action was really needed. The (i) first of these measures was a reduction of the State demand on land, especially in Bombay, Madras and the United Provinces and a limitation of that demand all over India; (ii) Next, a resolute attempt must be made to rescue the Indian agriculturist from the load of debt that overwhelmed him; (iii) These two measures must be accompanied by a third measure viz., the providing of facilities which, while encouraging thrift, will enable the agriculturist to borrow on occasions for his reasonable wants at a low rate of interest; (iv) Promotion of scientific agriculture, and (v) extension of irrigation were two other measures to which Government had already been paying attention; (vi) The promotion of industrial and technical education was also an urgent necessity as a remedy for the extreme poverty of the people; (vii) Then followed the spread of primary education, it being made free in all schools throughout India. This suggestion contains the germ of the primary education Bill which Mr. Gokhale brought before the Viceregal Council a few years later; (viii) The last suggestion was in connection with the pressing need of works of sanitary improvement, such as good water supply and drainage.

One would remark with regard to this programme of reform: "It is all right though a good deal ambitious. But where are the funds to come from?" And Sir Arundel, for instance, said in his budget speech that the advocacy of universal free primary education 'would be a large order' and that the first and the greatest difficulty was money. To people unaccustomed to such big schemes of reform, Mr. Gokhale's programme was bound to appear as extravagant and impracticable. But he was not daunted by the formidable character of the proposed undertakings, and stated that even as India's resources stood, there was room for undertaking all his measures. "Thus if the Army Reorganization scheme is held up or at least its initial cost is met out of borrowings, a sum from one to two millions a year will be available and that may be devoted to a vigorous extension of primary education. The profits of coinage—averaging now about two millions a year—may supply funds for the relief of agricultural indebtedness. The famine grant, which stands at a million sterling, may, after deducing the expenditure on actual famine relief, now be devoted to industrial and technical education. The deposits in Savings Banks may be made available to co-operative credit societies. And whatever surpluses accrue, may be devoted to assisting local bodies in the construction of works of sanitary improvement." This programme was calculated to dismay the official mind accustomed to moving in a narrow groove, and though the Hon'ble Mr. Baker expressed the keenest sympathy with every one of the above objects, he was afraid there were serious difficulties in the way and the remedies were open to serious objection.

V. Swadeshi.

The partition of Bengal, carried out in the teeth of popular opposition and protests in the Province, the general unsympathetic tone of the closing portion of Lord Curzon's administration and his utterances and measures which tended to disparage educated Indians, roused a storm of discontent in the whole country. The 'boycott' was used as a political weapon in Bengal and the Swadeshi movement was started as an economic measure calculated to promote the growth of indigenous industries. Whatever justification there was for the boycott movement in the provocation which Bengal had received and whatever merit it possessed as a temporary measure adopted to rouse the attention of the British public to the partition grievance, few people believed even at that time that it could be a normal feature of our relations with England. It was otherwise with the Swadeshi movement which was both a patriotic and an economic movement. In his presidential address at the Benares Congress, Mr. Gokhale analysed the whole political and economic situation and pointed out in a very lucid manner what the Swadeshi movement was and what it ought to be. It was a movement which had immense possibilities of good to the country if it was carried on in the right spirit. "The question of production", he said "is a question of capital, enterprise and skill, and in all these factors our deficiency at present is very great. Whoever can help in any one of these fields is, therefore, a worker in the Swad eshi cause and should be w comed as such. Not by methods of exclusion but by those of comprehension, not by insisting on every one working in the same part of the field but by leaving each one free to select his own corner, by attracting to the cause all who are likely to help and not alienating any who are already with us, are the difficulties of the problem likely to be overcome. Above all, let us see to it that there are no fresh divisions in the country in the name of *Swadeshism*. No greater perversion of its true spirit could be imagined than that". As a movement, on its material side, intended to promote, in every possible way, the growth of industries in India, by the patronage people were expected to extend to goods of Indian manufacture, and by the spirit of enterprise they were to display, Swadeshi was a national endeavour of the highest importance to the progress of this country.

In an address Mr. Gokhale delivered at Lucknow in the second week of February, 1907, he took the Swadeshi movement as the theme of his remarks and examined the industrial position of India from every point of view. That a resolve to patronise indigenous articles in preference to foreign, even at a sacrifice, will create a demand for Swadeshi commodities and thus render material assistance in the starting of new industries in India, is obvious. This is, however, only a part of the Swadeshi programme. It is calculated to accord to indigenous industries a measure of protection, in the shape of an assured custom, that cannot he expected from the State wedded to free trade principles. But its limitations have to be frankly recognized. Our industries are confronted with foreign competition which, owing to our lack of capital, enterprise, knowledge and other essentials, is bound to tell upon the success of Swadeshi concerns with patriotic enthusiasm alone to back them. In the situation as it exists, the industrial development of India is surrounded with grave difficulties and therefore the movement, if carried on with patience and circumspection, must be very slow and often very discouraging. In the speech referred to above, Mr. Gokhale took a comprehensive review of the situation, marked with high hopes about the industrial future of India and the part the people could play in shaping it, and observed :—" But, after all is said and done, I want you to recognise that the possibilities in the near future are not very large. I say this not to damp any one's enthusiasm because I do want that your enthusiasm should sustain itself at its highest glow in this matter. But remember that the competition before us is like that between agiant and a dwarf. Even if we successfully make up our minds to have nothing to do with foreign goods, even then the industrial salvation of India will not have been accomplished". In bringing the budget debate to a close on 28th March, 1906, Lord Minto referred to this question of Swadeshi in the following words :—

"The wealth, the welfare, the strength of a country that would hold its own in the world must depend largely upon the employment of its manhood in the development of its own resources. But now-a-days, in these days of rapid and easy transport, and in the face of our system of open markets, the home producer and home manufacturer must be prepared to face foreign competition or to fail. I am afraid he cannot expect his fellow countrymen for the sake of patriotism to buy his goods if they are inferior and more expensive than goods from other lands and I say to the supporters of Swadeshi,—that much abused word—that if 'Swadeshi' means an earnest endeavour to develop home industries in our open market for the employment and for the supply of the people of India, no one will be more heartily with them than my-self. But if by Swadeshi is meant an inability to recognise the signs of the times, a mistaken desire to maintain industrial systems long out of date, to create false markets by prohibiting the people of India from the purchase of better and cheaper goods, it will have no sympathy from me."

This was all very well so far as it went, though it was an aspect of the important problem which it was necessary to bear in mind, and it would have to be put down as a pious platitude. The difficulties are there, the competition is there; we have our failings and disadvantages. How shall we overcome them and what will the State do to lift the people out of their degraded and depressing condition, that to us always was and is, even at the present moment, the momentous problem. So far, there is practically no satisfactory reply, and we go on from day to day deploring our helpless situation and waiting for things to take a favourable turn. We referred, at the beginning of this chapter to the character of the new epoch which commenced with the close of Lord Curzon's regime. New ideas, political, social and economic, were spreading in the land, and the relations between the Government and the educated classes were not quite what they should have been. In view of the seriousness of the situation, Mr. Gokhale addressed the following appeal to Government :—

"More over, My Lord, the whole East today is throbbing with a new impulse, vibrating with a new passion and it is not to be expected that India alone should continue unaffected by changes that are in the very air around us. We could not remain outside this influence even if we would. We would not so remain if we could. I trust the Government will read aright the significance of the profound and far-reaching change which is taking place in the public opinion of the country. A volume of new feeling is gathering, which requires to be treated with care. New generations are rising up, whose notions of the character and ideals of British rule are derived only from their experience of the past few years, and whose minds are not restrained by the thought of the great work which England has on the whole accomplished in the past in this land. I fully believe that it is in the power of the Government to give a turn to this feeling, which will make it a source of strength and not of weakness to the Empire. One thing, however, is clear. Such a result will not be a achieved by any methods of repression. What the country needs at this moment above every thing else is a Government, national in spirit though it may be foreign in personnel, a Government that will enable us to feel that our interests are the first consideration with it and that our wishes and opinions are to it a matter of some account."

VI. Reforms Conceded.

There were several gratifying features about the budget for 1907-08, and they made it clear that the Hon'ble Mr. Baker was more responsive to popular demands pressed in the Viceregal Council than his predecessors. In the first place, there was a further reduction effected in the duty on salt and it was brought down to a uniform rate, in India and in Burma, of Re. 1 per maund. The first reduction to Rs. 2 a maund was made with effect from 1903-04, the second to Rs. 1-8 in 1905-06. Excluding Burma, which was not affected, the consumption increased by 9,68,000 maunds in 1903-04, 15,97,000 maunds in 1904-05 and 13,32,000 maunds in 1905-06. The latest measure of reduction was calculated to involve a sacrifice of revenue to the extent of 190 lakhs of rupees in 1907-08. The steadily increasing consumption of salt with each reduction of duty, completely established the fact that a high rate of duty entailed serious privation and suffering upon the poorer classes of the people. The Finance Member, of course, repeated the orthodox official view in the matter that the tax did not press with undue severity even on the poor and that the salt tax was the only contribution towards the public expenditure that was made by a large number of the people. Mr. Gokhale disputed the correctness of the latter statement as the increased consumption of salt had proved the incorrectness of the first. He maintained that the poorer classes made their fair contribution to the revenues of the State through the land revenue, excise, customs, stamps &c. The Finance Member would, of course, regard land revenue as rent and not tax* which was not correct, and discounted largely the contribution of the poorer

* See the Author's "Indian Administration": Chapter on Land Revenue.

classes as being negligible. The principle of Mr. Gokhale's suggestions with regard to the method of showing certain items of income and expenditure in the financial statement was accepted and one of them was actually adopted.

The reduction of the special grant of over two millions a year for the Army Reorganization scheme by half a million sterling, was another interesting feature of the budget for 1907-08. Mr. Gokhale pleaded with what appeared even to him as tiresome repetition for a reduction in Army expenditure and objected to reorganization schemes being financed from current revenues. He reiterated his plea, he said, with the full consciousness that it would not influence Government's policy but he did it, at the same, as a duty of one who represented the view of the Indian public. His arguments with respect to the improved political situation in Asia, the unjust burden of military expenditure thrown upon India, andthe wrong inflicted upon all classes of people by tneir being indiscriminately kept compulsorily disarmed, had made His Excellency the Commander-in-Chief a little impatient, and with reference to his remarks Mr. Gokhale observed:—"But My Lord, is it *my* fault that things have to be pressed again and again on the attention of the Government? If His Excellency would like to hear less of these complaints, the remedy lies to a certain extent in his own hands. A way must be found out of the present situation, which is no doubt difficult and delicate but which must not be allowed to continue as it is, simply because it is difficult and delicate." Another encouraging item in the budget was an increase in the provision for expenditure on education. The Finance Member made a somewhat hopeful reference to the desire of Government to deal favourably with the popular demand for free primary education. Mr. Gokhale was rather too sanguine about the significance of this statement and referred a little exultantly to the remark of Sir Arundel in the previous year as to the demand about free primary education being a large order. "What was, however, 'a large order,' in March became a very reasonable order in November, so reasonable indeed that the circular letter addressed to Local Governments on the subject showed unequivocally that the Government of India had already made up its mind to adopt the measure." He went to the length of saying that as the Government had already advanced so far, they ought not to delay long the taking of the next step viz., that of making a beginning in the direction of compulsory education. Experience was to show that all this was a bit premature.

Another measure of financial reform announced in the financial statement was the system devised to assist the Local Governments to meet famine expenditure which had, till then, to be met out of their limited assigned revenues. The Hon'ble Mr. Logan had complained about this on behalf of the Government of Bombay and the scheme now devised was this:—"The ruling principle of the scheme is to enable each Local Government whose territories are liable to famine, gradually to build up a reserve of credit with the Imperial Government on which it will be at liberty to draw when it becomes necessary to incur expenditure on famine relief. The means of creating this reserve of credit will be provided from Imperial revenues, in the form of an increase to the annual fixed assignment of each Local Government."* If owing to the severity or the widespread character of a famine the reserve of credit was exhausted, any further expenditure was to be shared equally between the Imperial and the Local Governments, instead of being wholly a Provincial charge as before. In extreme cases further assistance might also have to be given to a Local Government and the matter was to be determined according to the circumstances of the occasion.

Opium revenue had always been an important asset of the finance of the Government of India, but that source of revenue it was now decided to sacrifice by definite stages. This decision affected Indian finance considerably. It was responsible for several windfalls to Government and also for additional taxation that became necessary on account of the prospect of the disappearance of all opium revenue. The people of China consumed our opium in large quantities and the Liberal Government when it came into power in Great Britain, resolved to wipe off the disgrace that India should have been

* Financial Statement for 1907-08.

making profits out of the degrading habit of a neighbouring nation. Proposals also came from the Chinese Government for the gradual reduction of the imports of Indian opium into China, *pari passu* with the gradual contraction of the production of opium in that country, the object in view being the eventual extinction of the opium habit among the Chinese. As evidence of the readiness of His Majesty's Government to receive the Chinese proposals in a sympathetic spirit, it was thought expedient to give effect, during 1907-08, to a reduction of sales of opium from 52,800 to 49,200 chests, and to a corresponding contraction of the area under cultivation. The loss of revenue during the year was estimated at a little less than one crore of rupees. The Finance Member looked at the gradual extinction of the opium revenue with equanimity owing to the elasticity of Indian finance. He was not unaware of the other consequences to India of the acceptance of the Chinese proposals. "The economic loss to the country occasioned by the proscription of a valuable crop and an important industry; the contraction of our exports by the exclusion of a staple valued at over 9 crores a year, and its effect on our balance of trade; and the loss inflicted upon the people and Durbars of the poppy-growing States in Malwa"—all these considerations deserved the most anxious consideration. But the Finance Member thought that if all went on well, there was nothing worse to fear than the absorption for a few years of the means of affording further relief to the tax-payer and of incurring useful expenditure for the development of the country.

This was not a small sacrifice for India to make. Mr. Gokhale, however, reconciled himself to having such a big hole made in the revenues of India—the net opium revenue in 1906-07 was about 5½ crores of rupees—on the ground that it was an unholy gain. He said that he had always felt a sense of deep humiliation at the thought of this revenue, deiived as it was practically from the degradation and moral ruin of the people of China and he rejoiced that the stain was going to be wiped off. Mr. Baker was optimistic as to the future of Indian finance and relied upon the elasticity which our ordinary revenues had exhibited. During the five years beginning with 1903-04, he pointed out, the various reductions of taxes and abolition of cesses, involved a sacrifiee of revenue not far short of 6½ crores a year, and these measures were accompanied by the provision, out of Imperial revenues alone, of 105 lakhs per annum for Police reform, 80 lakhs per annum for Education, 24 lakhs per annum for Agricultural development and over 60 lakhs per annum for grants-in-aid of District and Local Boards.

VII. Railways and Currency.

The Financial Statement referred, in an apologetic tone, to the inability of Government to provide more than 13½ crores of rupees for railways and to the disappointment with which the reduction would be viewed by the commercial public. It went on to explain that as the railways were constructed mainly from loan funds and to a small extent form surplus revenues and other minor sources, the difficulty of borrowing on a large scale in the existing conditions of the money market, was responsible for the limited character of the funds made available for this purpose. On the other hand, public opinion viewed with disfavour the way in which ambitious schemes of railway construction were undertaken, year after year, and Mr. Gokhale urged that the claims of reforms like that of sanitation, were infinitely stronger and more urgent than those of railway construction. The clamour of those who wanted Government to finance more ambitious programmes of railway construction, led it at last to lay its hands upon a part of the profits from the coinage of rupees to provide the necessary funds. But for a long time, everything about the Gold Standard Reserve was uncertain and no one could say what its limits should be and how exactly it should be utilized. Pointedly asked by Mr. Gokhale to state the position clearly, the Finance Member declined the invitation to make an announcement of the intentions of Government as to the purposes and limits of the Reserve. Government was obviously groping in the dark and feeling its way. Ultimately it was found that it had drifted into a currency policy which was not in consonance with the recommendations of the Fowler Committee. The currency system, as it prevailed at this time, was supposed to be based on those recommendations and guided by the principles underlying them. But as the Chamberlain Commission expressly stated, the policy pursued by Government was a distinct departure from those principles, and in fact, it was impracticable and perhaps undesirable to stick to them. Whether the Indian standard should be a real gold standard or a gold-exchange standard, whether a gold currency should accompany that standard or had nothing to do with it, in what shape and where the gold reserve should be maintained and how it should be utilized for its main purpose—these and many other questions arose and demanded solution. The outcry against the currency policy of Government became so loud and the demand for an inquiry so insistent that a Royal Commission had at last to be appointed. But some years of further complaint and waiting had to pass before it became impossible to resist the demand any longer.

It was clearly understood that the profits on coinage were to be set apart in the gold standard reserve fund and were not to be devoted to any other purpose than that of supporting exchange but in the difficulty experienced in providing the large funds required for the annual railway programme, Government diverted these profits to railways. Thus in the financial statement for 1908-09, the Finance Member stated:—"The original estimates for the current year (1907-08) provided for 9 millions of capital expenditure (on railways). Later on, however, on the advice of the Railway Finance Committee, it was decided to increase this by another million, the additional funds being provided from the profits on coinage." For 1908-09 again, 10 millions were provided, and the Hon'ble Mr. Apcar said*:—"My Lord, as regards Railways and Railway Finances, I have to congratulate the Hon'ble Member on the fact that he was able after all to provide 15 crores for railway capital expenditure during 1907-08 and on his having provided for a 15 crore programme for 1908-09. At the same time it is to be regretted that there should have been any question as to whether this amount of money would be provided or not." He was not content even with this big programme and observed:—"Although I rejoice to see that the 15 crore programme is to be worked to for 1908-09, I believe that it is extremely doubtful whether a 15 crore programme is sufficient and whether we do not now require for the Railway works in India a 20 crore or even a larger programme." Many questions of this nature regarding the working and financing of the railways arose and the Secretary of State referred them to a special committee in London.

VIII. Budget for 1908-09.

The outstanding future of the financial statement for 1908-09 was the famine which was wide spread over a large part of Northern India and some other tracts elsewhere. Comparing this famine, however, with the calamities which occurred at the close of the last century, the Finance Member was able to

* Budget speech, 1908-09.

state that the situation was less serious than in 1897-98 or 1900-01 and that the financial position was also stronger than in those years. The lessons of the two famines of the past decade, said he, had not been lost on the Government. The machinery for combating distress had been brought to a higher pitch of efficiency and it had become a primary canon with it to issue takavi advances on the most liberal scale the moment famine was certain. On account of the adverse conditions, remission of taxation or the taking in hand of schemes of reform involving expenditure, was not to be thought of. The situation will be found reflected in the following figures :—

	Revenue	Expenditure	Surplus.
1906-07	£	£	£
(Accounts)	73,144,554	71,535,179	1,589,375
1907-08 (Revised Estimates	70,989,200	70,753,800	235,400
1908-09 (Budget Estimate)	73,438,900	72,867,400	571,500

Various changes effected in the form of accounts were announced in the financial statemeut, particularly the one Mr. Gokhale had been pressing for viz. the complete exclusion of the accounts and estimates of District and Local Boards from the Imperial budget and the statements appended thereto. This was in accordance with the practice in the

United Kingdom, where the income and expenditure of county councils are kept entirely separate from the public accounts. The reduction of the area under poppy cultivation and of the number of opium chests to be exported to China, was continued and was responsible for a diminution in the budgeted receipts.

A gratifying feature of the financial statement was the allotment of a sum 30 lakhs per annum to the different Provinces for expenditure on sanitary improvements with special reference to the prevention of plague. It was admitted that comparatively little had been done in the direction of the improvement of the public health and Government realised how the fact that no organized effort was made to improve the sanitary conditions in which the people lived, was made a reproach against it. The Provincial Governments were left free to decide how they would assist municipal bodies in undertaking works of sanitary improvement, with the funds thus placed at their disposal. During the five years 1902-03 to 1906-07, the amounts contributed by the several Provincial Governments as grants-in-aid to municipalities towards capital outlay on drainage and water works, came to an annual average of $3\frac{1}{8}$ lakhs for the whole country. Mr. Gokhale contrasted this paltry figure with the large amounts which had been provided for expenditure on the Army and the Railways out of current revenues. This treatment of sanitation, said Mr. Gokhale, as though the Government had no responsibility in regard to it, was one of the most melancholy features of the prevalent arrangement of financial decentralization under which sanitation had been made over to Local Bodies as their concern though they had admittedly no resources for undertaking large projects of improvement.

In this connection of the improvement of sanitation, the question of the utilization of surpluses came forward once more. It had been argued that surpluses being so very uncertain, they could not be depended upon as a source from which to finance schemes of sanitary reform. Mr. Gokhale did not see why it should be difficult to set aside the surpluses as they arose, in a separate fund and to place them at the disposal of the Local Governments for carrying out definite schemes. On the other hand, he regarded the practice of devoting surpluses to railway construction as unjust to the tax-payers and wholly indefensible. "What will the Hon'ble Member think" he asked, "of a man who while his children are sickening and dying, neglects to improve the sanitation of his house and uses whatever money he can spare out of his income for purposes of investment? He repeated that surpluses were so much more revenue taken from the people than was necessary for the requirements of the Government and as it was not possible to return a surplus directly to the people it ought to be spent in meeting non-recurring expenditure most urgently needed for their welfare. In view of the Finance Member's decision to devote to railway construction a sum of $1\frac{3}{4}$ millions sterling out of cash balances, he also raised the question whether there should not be a definite limit to these balances. Mr. Gokhale rubbed in his principle of financial administration that conditions in India required that a larger portion of the revenues should be devoted to objects on which the moral and material well-being of the masses ultimately depends. There were so many most urgent needs, and it was the obvious duty of the State to provide for them. The plea of the lack of funds Mr. Gokhale did not believe in. The money is there, he said, for whatever developments may take place immediately, and it can be found without difficulty as we go along if the burden is distributed over a number of years and the task taken in hand in a resolute spirit.

The attitude of the Finance Member, though sympathetic, was one of absolute *non-possumus* in this matter. To Mr. Gokhale's principle of financial management referred to above, the Hon'ble Mr. Baker opposed his own viz., that "current expenditure shall be met from current revenue." This major premise being accepted, it followed as a logical conclusion that sanitation being current expenditure, it must be financed from current revenue, and not from windfalls. He said:—"But it is not sound finance to attempt as a regular procedure to provide funds for a permanent and a continuing public service from sources which are necessarily spasmodic and precarious. When a surplus does occur, it cannot, as a rule, be more usefully applied than in reduction of the national debt which is the residuary legatee of all moneys not required for current expenditure."

IX. The Exchange Trouble.

Since the gold value of the rupee was artificially raised and fixed at 16 d., the exchange presented no difficulty and had a smooth course. In the midst of the uncertainty about the principles of the Indian currency system, which had given rise to an animated controversy, the organization, however, received a rude shock at the close of the year 1907. People had almost forgotten the time when the exchange was a potent factor of disturbance to Indian trade and finance, and they had settled down into ease and security. The experience of 1907-08 roused them into thinking on currency matters, and the subject provided food for reflection during the few succeeding years. Towards the close of 1907, owing to insufficient rain and the failure of certain crops, exchange became weak and there was little demand for Council bills. "Before the beginning of November, therefore, the conditions for a week and stagnant exchange were fully established. The jute trade was inactive; the wheat trade was doomed; cotton was somewhat uncertain; and much of the Burma rice might have to be diverted to India instead of going abroad. To these conditions there was suddenly superadded an external complication as serious as it was unforeseen. On the 20th October, the Mercantile National Bank of the United States of America was annonnced to be in difficulties; several big Trust companies fell in its wake;

and by the beginning of November a big financial crisis had developed in the United States."* The effects of this crisis were felt immediately in London where the Bank of England had to raise its rate to 7 per cent.—a rate which had not been experienced since 1873. Large quantities of gold were drained into America and great stringency was felt throughout the world. India could not expect to escape from the effects of the situation. The exchange steadily fell, for a time the Secretary of State withdrew from the market and the rupee touched the lowest point on 25th November when exchange dropped to 1-3$\frac{11}{16}$. The gold export point had been passed and the demand for gold increased and became insistent.

Government was approached with a view to ascertaining whether it would issue gold freely *i. e.*, without limit of amount, in exchange for rupees at Rs. 15 to one £. It paid anxious thought to the subject and considered its position very carefully. Its stock of gold was limited and was likely to be soon exhausted. Then it would have been compelled to discontinue the issues of gold with the inevitable result of precipitating a panic. Government therefore decided not to issue gold in larger quantities than £ 10,000 to any individual on any one day. The Secretary of State, who had stopped the sale of Council Bills, released gold from the currency chest in London in small quantities to

* Financial Statement for 1908-09

meet his needs, and it was decided that if exchange fell again below gold export point, Telegraphic Transfers on London should be offered for sale in India at a fixed price. This arrangement remained in force till the end of February 1908, but no occasion arose to put it into operation. The policy thus followed had its effect in raising the exchange towards the close of November and during December. Government was criticised for having refused to issue gold for export without limit, but it defended itself on the ground that its stock of gold was extremely small and that the gold was wanted not merely to redress any temporary defect in the balance of Indian trade but also directly or indirectly to supply demand from America which had already absorbed 23 millions sterling, and was only restrained from further inroads on the London market by reason of an abnormally high bank rate. The trouble over the adverse exchange was not, however, over in February 1908, as was thought. The financial depression in America and elsewhere checked the foreign demand for our jute, and cotton was not satisfactory. Owing mainly to the weakness of these staples, the last six months of the financial year, 1907-08, showed a net import of the value of 3·22 crores as against a net export value of 16·15 crores for the corresponding period in 1906–07. While our imports continued, the exports were checked by the unfavourable conditions in India, and on 25th March, 1908, exchange dropped below specie point. The readiness of Government to sell sterling bills on London was announced, and during the five months, April--August, 'reverse Councils' were sold to the extent of £ 8,008,000. The value obtained for the bills was paid into the silver branch of the Gold Standard Reserve and the Secretary of State made corresponding withdrawals of gold from the Reserve in London. The position steadily improved towards the close of the year and the exchange rose. A noticeable feature of this period of crisis was the exhaustion of the Government supply of gold. When the trouble began in October, 1907, Government held £ $4\frac{1}{4}$ millions in its currency chests, but no gold was coming into the country and the stock was depleted till at last it stood at only £100,000 in the beginning of 1909. There was no increased outflow of gold to meet the external demand partly because the inflow was stopped and also because "the comparative absence of the banking habit in the country makes it impracticable to collect with promptitude large quantities of gold even when they could be exported at a profit."

The experience through which we passed during the crisis, led people to criticise the financial and currency policy of Government, much of which appeared to them not very consistent with sound principle. The management of the Gold Standard Reserve, the diversion of a part of the profits on rupee coinage to railway construction and the decision to hold 6 crores of the Reserve in silver, led to the belief that 'opportunism rather than sound economic-principle dictated the policy of Government,' and the appointment of a commission to inquire into the question, began to be strongly urged. Sir Guy Fleetwood Wilson, who presented his first financial statement in 1909, expressed the view that India had a number of commissions lately and she deserved a rest. 'Commissions are always expensive, not always conclusive, and are usually somewhat unsettling bodies, and the one thing that our currency policy requires,' he said, 'is that it should be allowed to settle down into regular habits.' He admitted that the events of 1907 and 1908 had thrown a vivid searchlight upon India's currency policy and it was incumbent on the Government to see that the results were not lost sight of. He held, however, that the situation during the crisis had been resolutely and properly handled and the result was such that no one needed to be ashamed of it.

X. Problem of High Prices.

If the currency policy of Government thus strongly agitated the public mind, the steady rise of prices which was associated with it, attracted greater attention in the country. The advisability of appointing a strong committee to inquire into the question was urged from all quarters. The National Congress and the presse choed the public feeling. After some hesitation and delay Mr. K. L. Datta of the Finance Department was deputed to collect facts and opinions in the matter and to make a report. We now know how his inquiry led Mr. Datta to conclude that the rise in the price of food stuffs was the result of the failure of their production and supply in India to keep pace with the growth of population and how the price levels in this country were affected by the rise of prices that had taken place everywhere outside. He thought that the intimate contact of India with the world's markets, her exports of large quantities of raw materials and her gold standard, combined with the deficiency in the production of food grains as compared to the increase of population, were sufficient to account for the rise of prices in this country. The Government of India, while agreeing with Mr. Datta in other respects, would not endorse his proposition about the insufficient supply of food grains.* Mr. Gokhale was, however, one of those who thought that the phenomenally heavy coinage of new rupees during the preceding few years by the Government, had something to do with the general rise in prices. He did not ignore the influence of the rise of gold prices of commodities all over the world upon the price level in India, but contended that the extraordinary phenomenon in India could not be explained by that cause, and the coinage statistics threw an important light in the problem. The gross outturn of rupees at the Indian mints was as follows :—

	Crores.
1902-03	11·27
1903-04	16·17
1904,05	10·88

* See Government of India's Resolution on the subject, dated 24th October, 1914.

	Crores.
1905-06	19·60
1606-07	15·37
1907-08 (Estimate)	17·30

The following figures give the annual average of rupees coined *minus* old rupees recoined by the Government of India, for each decade from 1834 to 1893 when the mints were closed and for the years following the passing of the Act of 1899 when coinage operations on a large scale were resumed :—

Period (Annual Average for).	Crores.
1835-44	2·2
1845-54	2·4
1855-64	8·2
1865-74	4·8
1875-84	6
1885-93	8·3
1900-04	8·3
1905-08	20·6

After the mints were closed in 1893, the melting of rupees, which must have taken place on a pretty considerable scale before, ceased owing to the great difference between the intrinsic and the face value of the token coin. The stock of rupees in existence in India before 1898 was estimated at 130 crores and during the next ten years Government made a net addition to that stock, of over 100 crores. It is obvious that such a sudden inflation of the country's currency must have contributed to a rise of prices. This argument was, however, met with the fact of the increased industrial activity of the country, and it was urged that the augmentation of the currency was necessitated by the requirements of trade. Mr. Gokhale, however, showed by means of statistics that trade had not expanded at the same rate as the stock of the currency, and went on to say :—"What is probably happening is this. The rupees issued by the Government in response to the demands of trade go into the interior and spread themselves among those from whom purchases are made. But owing to various circumstances, they do not flow back quickly to centres of trade or to banks, and thus new rupees have to be obtained for transactions for which old rupees might have sufficed. Meanwhile, the melting back of rupees into silver having ceased, every issue becomes a net addition to the volume of the currency. If this analysis of the situation is correct, it suggests a grave problem, for it means that prices will tend to rise still further."

The Hon'ble Mr. Baker made a lengthy reply to Mr. Gokhale's case with regard to the connection between currency and high prices. In the first place, he doubted the accuracy of the figures representing the comparative addition made to the stock of rupees in circulation during the 15 years before and after the closing of the mints. According to him, whereas, on an average, 15 crores of rupees were coined annually in the former period, only 7 crores a year were coined in the second. And though the public would not melt rupees after their value had been artificially raised, there was the annual wastage, growing with the increase of population, and the recoinage of old defaced and light weight rupees by the Government. The rupees that were coined from year to year, were coined to meet the demand of the trade and were not redundant, and Mr. Baker repeated a dictum of Sir Clinton Dawkins, viz. that 'as long as Government refrains from coining rupees except upon the demand of trade, there can be no dilution of the currency.' He, therefore, concluded that there was absolutely no connection between high prices and the rupees in circulation in India. There would be no excess of currency over the demand for it from the public. Though there was no such provision in India as exists in other countries, for the export of the surplus if there was a redundancy of the curreney, as the rupee was a mere token, still the Government had provided an outlet viz. the sale of sterling bills on London when rupees were presented to it. Surplus rupees would thereby be effectively withdrawn from circulation till the redundancy had ceased. In short, Mr. Baker found no reason to suppose that the level of prices in India had been raised by the issue of rupees, and stated that the rise might be due to several local causes or might be traced to the changes in the value of metallic money in the markets of the outside world.

Sir Guy Fleetwood Wilson held similar views. He said that Government also were affected by the high prices and were prepared to give their best consideration to any suggestions that might be made and that were based upon knowledge and accurate data. And he stated further:—"There are deeper causes than Government action at work. India by its adoption of a gold standard has been switched on to the currency guage of the rest of the world: and is undoubtedly bearing its share in the price fluctuations to which the rest of the world has been subject. This country is undergoing great economic changes and the change in money values is one of them. Whether the change will ultimately result for the good of India, it is difficult to say. We all hope so, and Government will gladly take any part that it prudently can take in forwarding that end." Mr. Gokhale would not leave things at that. He returned to the subject in his budget speech of 1909 and repeated that a phenomenal rise in prices that had taken place in India could not be accounted for on any theory than that of the inflation of the token rupee currency of this country. In spite of everything that Mr. Baker had said, there could be no doubt about the fact of the enormous additions which Government had made to the stock of rupees in circulation in India and such an inflation of the currency could not but raise the level of prices. Without going to the length of saying, as some have done, that "the heavy coinage operations carried on during the recent years have not had so much the object of meeting genuine demands of currency in view as to earn large profits on the coinage of rupees and transmit those profits to England," we may point out what Prof. Keynes has to say in this connection. He observes:—"A succession of years, in which there is a heavy demand for currency makes it less likely that the heavy demand will persist in the year following. The effects of heavy coinage are cumulative. The Indian authorities do not seem to have understood this. They were, to all appearances, influenced by the crude inductive argument that, because there was a heavy demand in 1905-06, it was likely that there would be an equally heavy demand in 1906-07; and when there actually was a heavy demand in 1906-07, that this made it yet more likely that there would be a heavy demand in 1907-08. They framed their policy, that is to say, as though a community consumed currency with the same steady appetite with which some communities consume beer."*

We give here a long quotation from Mr. Gokhale's budget speech of 1909, as it makes clear his position with respect to the causes of high prices. He said:—

"Last year, in the course of the budget debate, I ventured to express my apprehensions on this subject, and further consideration has only strengthened those apprehensions. I think the quantitative theory of money holds good much more in the case of a backward country like India than in those of more advanced countries. Variations in the prices of individual commodities may be due to variations in the demand for them or in their supply. But a more or less general rise of prices can only point to a disturbance of the currency. Such rise need

* See "Currency Organizations of India" Page 70.—Alakh Dhari.

not be uniform in the case of all commodities, for in the view which I am stating, prices are a function of three variables--currency, demand and supply, and any general rise resulting from a disturbance of the currency may be modified in particular cases by one or both of the other two factors. The whole question requires a close and immediate investigation by a competent body of men, and I sincerely trust the Government have made up their mind to direct such an enquiry......It has been urged in defence of the heavy coinage of rupees in recent years that they were issued solely to meet the demands of trade. The course adopted does not, however, seem to be justified by the results. It is important to remember that the Fowler Committee had expressed itself strongly and clearly against such new coinage until a sufficient quantity of gold was in circulation in the country. "The Government, they wrote, should continue to give rupees for gold, but fresh rupees should not be coined until the proportion of gold in the currency is found to exceed the requirements of the public." It seems to me that the only way now out of our difficulties is to follow the example of France and the United States, and while admitting the rupees to unlimited tender stop the coinage of new rupees and coin gold pieces instead. Of coure, I express this opinion with great diffidence, for there are serious considerations on the other side and the whole subject is enveloped in great obscurity. But I fear that the present half way house will not do and unless we place our currency on an automatic and self-adjusting basis, the clouds that are already overhead will thicken and not roll away."

But the Government drifted further and further and departed in fundamental points from the recommendations of the Fowler Committee. The Chamberlain Commission on Indian Finance and Currency only confirmed the policy into which the Government of India had drifted. The idea of a gold standard and a gold currency was abandoned and it was laid down that India did not want and require a gold currency. It was only a costly luxury and the token rupee was quite enough for the poor population of India. The maintenance of exchange at the fixed rate has thus come to be the only object of the Indian currency policy with which Government need concern itself. If gold is made available for remittance purposes, the State is supposed to have done its duty to the people. The appointment of the Chamberlain Commission itself was, however, necessitated by the dissatisfaction of the people with the policy which the Secretary of State and the Government of India had come to pursue in matters connected with the various features of our currency system.

XI. Last year of the Old order.

In 1909, the Morley-Minto reforms came into operation, but the budget debate in that year took place under the old system as the new Councils were yet to be constituted. It was also a year which succeeded a year of a deficit of $3\frac{3}{4}$ millions and a year the revenues and expenditure of which could be balanced with the greatest difficulty. Here is the position:—

	Revenue	Expenditure	Surplus (+) or Deficit (–)
	£	£	£
1907-08 (Accounts)	71,003,275	70,697,029	+ 306,046
1908-09 (Revised)	69,628,600	73,349,100	– 3,720,500
1909-10 (Budget)	73,750,900	73,520,000	+ 230,900

The shock of this deficit for 1908-09 was all the more severe on account of the fact that after a succession of surpluses extending over ten consecutive years, we came suddenly and almost without a warning, to a year of a heavy deficit, and this abrupt change was accompanied by an uncertainty about the future, which aggravated the situation. The Finance Member resolved to square the two sides of the account for the year 1909-10 by severe economy and not by addition of taxation. The outlook was far from cheerful, and Sir Guy Fleetwood Wilson was cautious in the language he used in the financial statement regarding the immediate future. There is one point which must be noted in this connection. In view of the times of deficits and depression through which India was passing. there was a tendency in certain quarters to ques tion the wisdom of the remissions of taxation which had been granted in past years. Mr. Gokhale removed the misapprehension by pointing out how the various remissions put together amounted to about 4 millions a year and just absorbed the saving, which the Government had made by the artificial raising of the exhange value of the rupee which came to about 3⅓ millions. And in spite of these remissions, the revenue stood in 1909 at a higher figure than six years before.

CHAPTER V.

COMMANDING POSITION.

I The Reformed Council.

With the year 1910, a new chapter was opened in the history of India, financial and political. What were the constitutional changes introduced under the Morley-Minto scheme of reform, it is not our purpose here to say.* In his speeches closing the budget debates in 1908 and 1909, Lord Minto had described how the proposals of reform had emanated from the Government of India and how they were intended to associate the people more intimately with the work of Government and thus to satisfy the legitimate aspirations of the people. Mr. Gokhale acknowledged in felicitous language the debt of gratitude which India owed to the two noble-hearted statesmen—Lords Morley and Minto and offered a personal explanation as to the part he had played in the shaping of the reform scheme. He pithily summed up the feeling of the Indian people when he said:—"My Lord, I sincerely believe that Your Lordship and Lord Morley have, between you, saved India from drifting towards what cannot be described by any other name than chaos. For, however strong a Government may be, repression can never put down the aspirations of a people and never will."

---

* See "Indian Administration": pages 122-123.

In his speech on the budget in 1909, the Hon'ble Mr. Baker had given a picturesque account of the evolution of the system of budget discussion, and Sir Guy Fleetwood followed him in 1910, adding a statement about the changes in that system inaugurated in that year.

" They may be summed up by saying that the discussion now extends over several days instead of one or two, that it takes place before instead of after, the budget is finally settled and that the members have the right to propose resolutions and divide the Council. The general order of the discussion of the financial statement i. e., a statement of the preliminary financial estimate for the next year, is as follows:—On an appointed day each year, the financial statement with an explanatory memorandum is presented to the Council by the Finance Member and no discussion of the same is allowed on that day. The first stage in the discussion commences, when, on a subsequent day duly appointed, the statement is taken duly into consideration and any member may move a resolution relating to any alteration in taxation, any new loan or any additional grant to Local Governments proposed. The second stage commences when all the resolutions which may be moved, are disposed of. A resolution may now be moved with reference to any question covered by a head or group of heads specified in the statement and introduced by the Member in charge. Certain subjects such as foreign relations and relations with Native States and matters under adjudication by a court of law and also certain heads of revenue such as customs, assessed taxes and State railways, army &c. are excluded from discussion. Finally, the Budget, i. e. the financial statement as finally settled by the Governor-General in Council, is presented to the Council by the Finance Member and on a subsequent day a general discussion on it takes place when no resolutions are allowed. The budget is not likewise put to vote."

II. Additional Taxation.

In the financial statement for 1909-10, Sir G. F. Wilson had been extremely cautious and not over-sanguine about the future. But no one ever thought that, after an interval of twelve months, with no extraordinary causes, he would propose the imposition of extra taxation upon the people. But that was the unpleasant surprise the Finance Member had for the country. After estimating the revenue and expenditure for 1910-11, he came to the conclusion that there was a gap between resources and requirements —a shortage of £ 1,127,000 due to opium and the new settlement with Eastern Bengal and Assam. He thought that the ordinary expenditure, though steadily growing, could have been met with the ordinary revenue, which was also expanding and he could thus have a normal budget, the two sides of the account just balancing each other. But the loss under Opium and the needs of Eastern Bengal, made equilibrium impossible and rendered a permanent strengthening of the resources inevitable. He therefore proposed that the bulk of the additional amount that was necessary, should be raised by increasing the customs duties on liquors, on tobaco, on silver and on petroleum. A small amount would also be secured by enhancing the stamp duties on certain instruments. Even with these additions, the financial position was not free from difficulties. It was Sir G. F. Wilson who characterised the Indian budget as 'a gamble in rain' on account of the fact of the monsoon being always a dominating factor in the forecasting of revenue and expenditure in this country. He concluded his financial statement with the following characteristic words :—" No right-minded man can impose additional taxation on India with a light heart. To me it is a very genuine sorrow to be obliged to do so. I did not sow the storm, but I am reaping the whirlwind."

The additional taxation necessitated an amendment of the Tariff Act of 1894, and when the Bill came before the Viceregal Council, Mr. Gokhale availed himself of the opportunity to offer a few observations on the general financial situation which had made the measure inevitable. The situation was peculiar, because it was the first time when it was proposed to levy additional taxation in a normal year, free from any specially disturbing factors. Till then fresh taxation was associated with war or famine or a sudden increase in military charges or a falling exchange. The Finance Member had thrown the responsibility for the extra taxation, as we have stated above, upon the Opium revenue whose life was threatened and whose existence was precarious. Mr. Gokhale protested against this view. The opium revenue was expected to go on steadily diminishing without affecting the financial position, and Sir Edward (then Mr.) Baker had expressly stated three years before,* that the normal increase in the revenues would be sufficient to make up the loss on opium. Government was then prepared to part with one-tenth of the opium revenue every year, according to the arrangements made with China. In view of the high price of the drug, the Finance Member had actually budgeted for a full 3½ millions, the amount realised in 1907-08 and yet opium was

* See page 170.

held responsible for the necessity of fresh taxation. Mr. Gokhale's explanation was that the expenditure of the Civil Departments and the railways was growing beyond proper limits and that was at the bottom of the whole trouble ; the dwindling opium revenue had been anticipated and would not have necessitated an addition to the burdens of the tax payer. It was hoped that fresh taxation would not be imposed until at least a policy of severe retrenchment had been carried out in all departments. "But," said Mr. Gokhale, "the forces that make for economy in this country are extremely weak, while those that make for continuous increases of expenditure in different departments, are enormously strong, and one of the greatest needs of the country is to devise measures which will effectively safe-guard the interests of economy." It was simply amazing that while the Finance Member proposed extra taxation on the ground that the money that would otherwise be raised, would be insufficient for current purposes, he had provided a sum of over three-fourths of a million sterling for the redemption of railway debt out of revenue ! As to the taxes proposed, Mr. Gokhale objected to two of them viz. those on petroleum and silver, the first falling upon the poor and the second on the indigenous cotton industry. He proposed instead an export duty on jute, which was justified by the fact that while the cotton industry of Bombay was taxed, the jute industry of Bengal was altogether free, and secondly, it was but just that Bengal should contribute to meet a deficit caused by increased cost of administration in Eastern Bengal.

The Hon'ble Mr. Meston strongly resented this criticism. He could not, however, pass it by as being easy and irresponsible, coming as it did from Mr. Gokhale, who was one of those whose advice stood upon a different footing. In particular, he did not like the manner in which the accuracy of the figures supplied by the Finance Department had been called in question. In his budget speech Mr. Gokhale vindicated his right to criticise financial estimates and observed:—"My Lord, this is in reality a small matter; but the statement made by the Hon'ble Mr. Meston, if allowed to remain uncontradicted, might cause serious inconvenience hereafter, because objection might again be taken to any suggestion as to under-estimates or over-estimates." It is interesting to notice how, in that speech, he again took a masterly review of the financial situation and compared it with the position with which Lord Dufferin's Government was confronted in 1886. He traced the embarassment of Government to the expenditure which had been allowed to grow on an enormous scale. He summed up the situation thus:—"The whole position therefore is this, that during the ten years 1898-1908, while six crores were remitted in taxation, the annual civil expenditure was allowed to grow by 15 crores and about 5 crores of additional expenditure was incurred every year in connection with the Army; this gives an increase of about 20 crores in civil and military expenditure in the course of ten years, or an average growth of 2 crores a year." He went on to suggest that Government should take credit only for a steadily diminishing opium revenue and arrange to keep all excess above that figure as a windfall or extraordinary revenue to be devoted to non-recurring expenditure. The irony of the situation was that while additional revenue was being raised by extra taxation, funds were not available for being devoted to objects intimately connected with the real well-being of the people such as primary and technical education, sanitation and relief of agricultural indebtedness. Mr. Gokhale, therefore, thought that an immediate inqiury into the growth of expenditure was called for.

III. Surpluses and Public Debt.

It has been stated above that the Council reforms of 1909 conferred upon members of Legislative Councils the right of moving resolutions on different matters and also on proposals made in the financial statement, with certain reservations.* And this newly acquired right Mr. Gokhale exercised fully and most beneficially, by moving a number of very useful resolutions on important matters. When the first stage of the discussion of the financial statement for 1910-11 was reached, Mr. Gokhale moved on 5th March 1910, the following resolution:—"That this Council recommends that the amount of loan to be raised during the year 1910-11, should be £ 1,245,000 instead of £ 1,000,000 and that the sum of £ 245,000 which is the estimated surplus for the

* See Section I of this Chapter.

current year should be allotted to the several Provincial Governments to be expended by them in assisting local bodies to carry out projects of sanitary improvements." The main object of the resolution was that the surplus of the current year, which would otherwise have gone to increase the cash balances of the Government and provide for capital expenditure, should be made available to Local Governments so that they might pass it on to local bodies, and especially municipalities, in carrying out projects of sanitary improvement. In the words of Mr. Gokhale, the resolution came to this that "all surpluses that are annually realised, whenever they are realised, should, instead of going into the cash balances, and from there going into the construction of railways, and indirectly to the redemption of unproductive debt, should be placed at the disposal of Provincial Governments and be earmarked to assist municipalities in the promotion of sanitation" He had pressed this question again and again on the attention of the Council for six years and except for the 30 lakhs granted by Sir Edward Baker, nothing had been done for the improvement of municipal sanitation. Railway construction and reduction of debt were all right, but in view of the more urgent needs, surpluses could not, without detriment to public good, be devoted to those objects. The Municipalities were extremely poor and their resources small. And the best way and the most feasible plan would be to place at their disposal the surpluses which might accrue from time to time.

The Hon'ble Mr. (now Sir James) Meston maintained the orthodox official view, which he regarded as a fundamental principle in modern finance, that 'any actual surplus of revenue over expenditure should be devoted to the redemption of public debt.' He admitted that revenue surpluses were used in reducing the amount of indebtedness, though in an indirect way and explained the position thus:—"That is to say, it saves us from borrowing an equivalent amount and to that extent keeps down the growth of our debt. Moreover, inasmuch as we spend on productive capital outlay in ordinary years considerably more than we borrow, the effect is that we always reduce our non-productive debt by the amount of our revenue surplus. That, of course, is simple enough. It simply means a short-cut in our accounts. Instead of using our revenue surplus to pay off non-productive debt and borrowing to the full extent for productive works, we borrow the net amount which we require and treat our revenue surplus as enabling us to make a corresponding transfer from non-productive to productive debt." He regarded this as a kind of national sinking fund and warned the Council against the principle laid down by Mr. Gokhale viz. that as the amount of our unproductive debt was extremely small, there was no need to reduce it by devoting surpluses to that purpose and no harm in borrowing for productive purposes.

We cannot resist the temptation of quoting here a fine passage in which Sir Guy Fleetwood

Wilson gave a lucid description of the nature of the Cash Balances of India, as it is calculated to make clear what otherwise is a very obscure subject. He said:—

"As the Government of India is its own banker, it is into our general cash balances that all our current revenue is paid, and from them that all our current expenditure is drawn. They are also the reservoir for the proceeds of all sterling and rupee loans, whether raised b Government or by railway companies which work our State lines; for the whole of our unfunded debt; and for all the miscellaneous deposits which are not earmarked for separate custody. All the Provincial balances merge in them, and in them are absorbed all the repayments and interest of State loans or advances to local bodies and private individuals. Similarly it is out of our cash balances that we take all our capital expenditure on railways and irrigation; all the advances which Government makes to local authorities and private persons; and all the money used in the discharge of our permanent, temporary or unfunded debt, or in the repayment of deposits. Finally, it is through our cash balances, owing to their being located partly in England and partly in India, that Council Bills are usually drawn and the greater part of Government's remittances between England and India effected. it is with our cash balances therefore that our estimate of ways and means are concerned."

Mr. Gokhale's reply to the Hon'ble Mr. Meston was effective. As to the reduction of the debt caused by famines, there was a special provision in each year's budget for the famine insurance grant. In the course of his speech, the Hon'ble member had made the following remark:—"Incidentally also it cannot have escaped the Hon'ble Mr. Gokhale's notice that the large surpluses which we have been able in recent years to use for the reduction of debt have represented in the main the net profits from our railways; and there is a certain fitness which,

I am sure, the Hon'ble Gentleman will recognise in employing for the building up of our magnificent railway property some part of the surplus income which it yields us." To this Mr. Gokhale replied that though he had not got the exact figures before him, he was sure that 'the Hon'ble Member was wrong.' For several years, the railways paid nothing and were a mere drain upon the resources of the country. "Moreover," he continued, "if you are going to point your finger to the profits from railways, I would ask you to remember that railways have cost us, ever since they were first built, I think 53 or 54 crores, not less, during the time that railways were a losing concern. Therefore, if you are making any small profits now, those profits, I venture to say, should go to repay the country for the losses the country had to bear on account of railways out of current revenues for 40 or 50 years." Mr. Gokhale asked the Council not to accept the view that had been put forward viz. that sanitation was the business of local bodies and that they must help themselves as well as they could.

IV. Two More Resolutions.

The Famine Insurance grant and Railway finance formed the subjects of two other Resolutions Mr. Gokhale moved in 1910. By the first he recommended that the annual allotment under Famine Relief and Insurance to Reduction or Avoidance of Debt should be abolished and by the second that the provision for the working expenses of State

Railways for the year 1910-11 should be reduced by one crore of rupees. Having given a lucid account of the origin of the Famine Relief Fund, the policy laid down by Government in connection with it and the use that had been made of that Fund, Mr. Gokhale contended that as the original purpose of that part of the Fund to be devoted to the reduction or avoidance of debt was not being fulfilled, it should be stopped and the money thus set free be made available for other important objects. During the period 1895 to 1910, the ordinary or unproductive debt of India had been reduced from 70 to 40 millions and out of this amount so reduced, the portion of the Famine Relief grant devoted to reduction, came to only 4½ millions. The debt thus being reduced independently of the grant, Mr. Gokhale urged, it was unnecessary that this sum of 4½ millions should have been further spent in the reduction of debt. It should be noted here that the half million is not directly devoted to the reduction of debt but is made available as capital for production purposes, chiefly railways and to that extent, the ordinary debt is taken as being reduced. Mr. Gokhale brought out his point by saying:—"It is true that Government devote this to the reduction of debt, but they devote it to the reduction of debt by increasing the amount available for productive purposes and principally railway construction. Therefore, this sum taken out of revenue, which is intended to mitigate the rigors of famine and which is also intended to enable the Government to borrow in times of famine, is being ordinarily devoted to increase the resources of Government for capital outlay on railway construction." The principle of the contention was the old one so often insisted upon by Mr. Gokhale viz. that current revenues should be spent on useful measures directly conducive to the bettering of the condition of the people and that the unproductive debt of India being extremely small, it was not necessary to be anxious about it to the extent of reducing it with current revenues. He disposed of the argument on the other side by saying emphatically that India did not want a Sinking Fund and that she must solve her own problems in her own way.

As to Railway finance, Mr. Gokhale's complaint was that since the institution of the Railway Board in 1905, the working expenses had mounted up from about 46 per cent. to 55 per cent. of the gross receipts. Sir Edward Baker had also made a similar complaint and it was suggested that the working expenses should be strictly limited. Sir T. Wynne, Chairman of the Railway Board, showed why the expenses had increased and how the expansion of trade and the needs of the public had necessitated the increase. Two remarks in Mr. Gokhale's reply were interesting and they show how he had come to acquire a fund of the inestimable quality of humour and ready wit. Argument he could promptly meet with cogent argument and figures with figures. But his touches, here and there, become very enlivening. He is no longer a mere economist and cold calculator but has also cultivated the style of delightful banter and repartee. Referring to an argument used by Sir T. Wynne, he remarked:—

> "The Hon'ble Member also said that, if this resolution were passed, it would be necessary to reduce the operative part of the expenses, and that might mean the dismissal of a number of my countrymen. Well, I am not really frightened by that. I find on looking up the lists here, that most of the men in the higher branches, at any rate, are the Hon'ble Member's countrymen and not mine, and if he were only to dismiss my countrymen, well, he would not get much out of that. If he wants to make a substantial reduction, he will have to get rid of some of his own countrymen."

The Hon'ble Malik Umar Hyat Khan, hailing from the Punjab, had opposed Mr. Gokhale's resolution on the ground that if money were not spent on railways, the grain in his province would not be carried away to the markets outside. With reference to this Mr. Gokhale observed:—

> "I will say only one thing more, and that is with regard to what the Hon'ble Malik Umar Hyat Khan said. The Hon'ble Member's faith in everything that the Government does is most touching: he stands by the Government even when the Hon'ble Sir Edward Baker criticises it. Nobody ever said that the grain in the Punjab should not be carried; the question is whether the expenditure which the Railway Board is incurring, whether all this increased expenditure, was required."

V. Growth of Expenditure.

Retrenchment and economy being the watchwords of Mr. Gokhale's financial policy, and finding that civil and military expenditure in India had been growing up unrestrained, while little attention was being paid to more urgent reforms like the spread of education, he missed no opportunity to expose this grievous defect in our financial arrangements, and in his budget speech of 1910, he reviewed the situation relating to the enormous increase of expenditure and observed :—"The whole position is this, that during the ten years 1898 to 1908, while six crores were remitted in taxation, the annual civil expenditure was allowed to grow by 15 crores and about 5 crores of additional expenditure was incurred every year in connection with the army; this gives an increase of about 20 crores in civil and military expenditure in the course of ten years, or an average growth of 2 crores a year. My Lord, everyone must admit that this is a phenominal increase, considering that the normal growth of revenue ordinarily has been estimated by a previous Finance Minister at about one crore and twenty lakhs. I think these figures suggested—to my mind they imperatively suggest—the necessity for an inquiry into the growth of civil and military expenditure during the last ten years." This need was all the greater owing to the steady decline in the opium revenue which the country had to face.

The whole position was this: while it was imperative that the strictest economy should be practised and expenditure should be cut down wherever possible, consistently with a decent measure of efficiency, of course, an increase, and even a very large increase of expenditure was called for on objects intimately connected with the real well-being of the people. And if retrenchment did not produce the money required for these objects, Mr. Gokhale would not shrink from advocating additional taxation for the purpose. He strongly felt that so extraordinary and disquieting a development of the financial situation demanded a close scrutiny, and early in 1911 he moved a resolution in the Viceroy's Council pleading for a public inquiry by a mixed body of officials and non-officials into the causes of the phenomenal increase in expenditure. The speech he made in support of this resolution was one of his greatest performances. His marshalling and handling of figures was simply marvellous and the spirit and powers of Mr. Gladstone could be easily traced in his exposition of the financial situation. He surveyed the field of Indian finance from 1875 to the year 1908-09, and divided this long period of 33 years into four smaller periods of more or less equal duration for comparing the growth of expenditure. He made very elaborate calculations to arrive at the normal net revenue and expenditure and to eliminate all the different factors such as exchange and remission of taxation, which were likely to render the comparison unfair. There were two facts to be borne in mind at the outset: (1) that out of the 51 millions that were available for ordinary expenditure every year, 30 millions were devoted to civil expenditure (6 millions for collection of revenue, 15 millions for the salaries and expenses of civil departments, about 5 millions for miscellaneous civil charges and about 4½ millions for civil works) and a little under 21 millions was spent on the Army; and (2) that this total real revenue, excluding opium receipts, was capable of growing at the rate of about 1½ per cent. per annum.

We give below in a tabulated form the results of Mr. Gokhale's survey:

Period.	Annual Increase of Revenue.	Annual Increase of Expenditure.
(1) 1875-1884	1¾ p. c.	⅔ p. c.
(3) 1884-1894	1½ p. c.	1½ p. c.
(3) 1894-1901	1½ p. c.	1½ p. c.
(4) 1901-02 to 1908-09.	2 p. c.	5 p. c.

The moral of these figures was obvious and pointed to an immediate and independent and a searching inquiry. There had been such inquiries in the past in 1874 by a Parliamentary Committee, in 1886-87 by Lord Dufferin's Committee and in 1897 by a Royal Commission presided over by Lord Welby. The time had come when a similar inquiry had become absolutely necessary. There were four remedies which, in Mr. Gokhale's opinion, were required by the situation. (1) What Mr. Gladstone used to call the spirit of expenditure and which was abroad in this country, must be chained and controlled and the spirit of economy installed in its place; (2) the Military expenditure must be substantially reduced; (3) there should be a more extended employment of the indigenous Indian agency in the public service; and (4) that provision should be made for an independent audit in this country. The reader will recognise in these remedies the suggestions which had been made to the Welby Commission and will see how even an interval of fourteen years had made no substantial change in the spirit of the Indian Administration.

Such a masterly speech could not but evoke more or less strong replies from the official side. It was also not a difficult matter for Mr. Gokhale to dispose of the arguments of his opponents. Mr. Meston and Sir Guy Fleetwood Wilson had, however, been so much impressed with the ability, the knowledge and the powers of exposition which he brought to bear upon the discussion of every question he took up, that they invariably treated him and his case with all possible respect and friendliness, though it was necessary for them to defend the official position. It is a pleasure to watch the friendly duels which took place between the chivalrous antagonists and to mark the commanding position which Mr. Gokhale had made for himself in the Imperial Legislative Council. It was a generous compliment, but one richly earned, which the Hon'ble Mr. Meston paid to him when he said in rising to criticise Mr. Gokhale's speech:—"My Lord, if he will permit me, I should like to begin by offering my congratulations to the Hon'ble Mover upon the lucidity and the extreme fairness with which he has placed this complicated case before the Council. Like the late Mr. Gladstone, the Hon'ble Mr. Gokhale has the rare and happy knack of making figures interesting, and it has been a sincere pleasure to listen to the skill with which he marshalled his figures and inspired life into the dry bones of our statistical returns." Mr. Gokhale had not the slightest difficulty in tearing the official defence to pieces. The Finance Member was most sympathetic and though he had his differences, he cordially agreed with Mr. Gokhale on several important points. Sir Guy has, in fact, been one of our most popular and sympathetic Finance Ministers. Extraordinarily capable, of generous instincts, and possessed of vast experience financial affairs, he had a high appreciation for Indians and sympathised with their aspirations. He concluded his remarks on the Resolution with the following words :—"Last year I extended to the Hon'ble Member my sympathy. This year I am able to go a step further. I am in agreement with him as to the object he has in view, but I disagree as to the method by which he proposes to arrive at the result we both wish to attain. Next year I may find salvation and whole-heartedly agree with him from first to last. On one thing we are all of one mind; that it is an intellectual treat to hear Mr. Gokhale give an exposition of his views. He and I seem to be proceeding not on parallel but on converging lines, and that is as it should be; for antagonism should have no place between a Finance Minister and Indian Members who desire the good of their country." Mr. Gokhale ultimately withdrew his resolution in view of the assurances which Sir Guy had given, and of the fact that Lord Hardinge having very recently assumed the reins of office, it was only fair that His

Excellency should have time to look into the question himself.

VI. Permanent Provincial Settlements:

The actual working of the *quasi* permanent settlements revealed the defects lurking in the arrangements which, it had been stated, had been invested in 1904, with a large measure of permanence, and were not to be revised except under certain special and extraordinary circumstances. On a review of the Decentralization Commission's report, the Government of India had to consider the whole question again, particularly as it had to readjust the arrangements with certain provinces soon after the settlements had been effected. In a comprehensive Resolution*, the Supreme Government reviewed the history of the development of decentralized finance and explained the principles of the permanent settlements which were made with the various Provincial Governments. In his financial statement for 1911-12, Sir G. F. Wilson also briefly but lucidly referred to this subject. It was stated that the financial settlement with each of the eight major Provinces was in future to be permanent, subject of course to the liability of the two parties to help each other in special emergencies. Certain stringent restrictions were imposed upon the Provincial Governments in the matter of their balances; they were not to budget for a deficit in current revenue and expenditure unless the excess of expenditure was one due to a wholly exceptional cause. If for a special and tem-

* Resolution of the Government of India of 18th May 1912.

porary reason any Local Government had exhausted its balances and received permission to overdraw, it would have to take a short loan from the Imperial exchequer and pay interest on it.

These restrictions were accompanied by certain favaurable features. In a good year, the Local Governments would share in the surplus which the Imperial Government might distribute. Moreover, if the fixed assignment of a Province became unduly high, it would be converted into a share of growing revenue. Finally, the Supreme Government would not exercise over the budgetary arrangements of the Local Governments the same minute control as in the past. "From a purely financial point of view, the immediate effect of these changes was to convert fixed assignments amounting to the imposing figure of 3½ crores a year into growing revenue. In this way the normal annual growth of its resources in each Province is brought much closer to the normal ratio of growth in its expenditure than has been possible in the past." Sir Guy spoke of it as a great reform calculated to stimulate provincial independence and self-reliance and to relieve the Government of India from unforeseen and indeterminate liability to which Imperial revenues were formerly exposed.

As we have observed in a previous chapter,* the permanent settlements have given satisfaction neither to the Local Governments nor to the people. In his budget speech, Mr. Gokhale noted four special

* See Pages 74–75.

characteristics of the new settlements : (1) There would be in future a withdrawal of all minute control over the budgets of Provincial Governments; (2) the doctrine of contractual responsibility would be enforced rigidly in the case of those Governments ; (3) that as far as possible, Provincial revenues would be derived from portions of growing revenues and that large fixed allotments would not be made; and (4) that a further step had been taken in the direction of the provincialization of certain revenues. They were all important changes, he said, no doubt ; but he doubted whether the new settlements would prove any more permanent than the last quasi-permanent settlements, or than even the old quinquennial settlements. The root of the mischief, according to him, lay in this that the Government of India had at its disposal too large a share of growing revenues and its expenditure was confined to the Army and a few services which were directly under it. There was thus a tendency to spend more and more on the Army and when surpluses accrued they were doled out to the Provincial Governments. These latter get into the habit of expecting the doles, and the expectation of doles is most demoralising. Mr. Gokhale's proposal, therefore, was that instead of receiving its whole income from growing revenues, the Government of India should receive large fixed contributions from Provincial Governments, say, upto about one-third or one-fourth of its revenues, the other two-thirds or three-fourths being derived from growing resources. He compared our system of finance with that in countries like Switzerland and Germany and urged that the process of decentralization should be completed and we should advance from that to federal finance, which should be our goal.

The Hon'ble Mr. Quin, representing the Government of Bombay, drew prominent attention to the more unsatisfactory features of the new settlements, viz. the utitization of special grants made to Provincial Governments, who wanted the old bonds of control loosened and not made more rigid in this matter; the interest that they were called upon to pay upon loans taken in times of stress from the Government of India; the withholding of the power of taxation from the Provincial Governments and of the power of borrowing in the local market. He said:—"The enlargement of the Provincial Councils, on which there is now a majority of non-officials, has effected radical change in its constitution, and the Government of Bombay have now at hand to assist it in matters of finance, a Council so composed as to be fully capable of successfully administering its own finances. This Council cannot be expected to attract and retain the best men unless it be given real power in respect of the finances of the Presidency and be permitted to exercise this power free from all checks and restrictions which are not absolutely essential to the maintenance of the general control of the Imperial Government." The Hon'ble Member thus gave voice to a feeling largely shared by Local Governments and the people and showed how the so-called

Permanent Settlements could not be really permanent until they gave more power and larger resources to the Provinces. As to the power of taxation, Mr. Gokhale admitted that Provincial finance could not attain an independent position unless and until that power were conferred upon the Provincial Councils, but he thought this could not be done in the absence of real popular control over provincial legislation. He said:—" I think, in the first place, the present practice of discussing Provincial Budgets must be well settled, and the public opinion in the different Provinces must make itself felt by the Provincial Governments much more than it is doing today. Secondly, before powers of taxation are conferred on Local Governments, it is necessary that every Local Government should be a Council Government, with a Governor at its head, coming fresh from England. And thirdly, it is necessary that there should be an elected majority of Members in these Councils. When this position is reached, I think powers of taxation may safely be entrusted to Provincial Councils, but till then I would keep those powers in the hands of this Council. Finally, as regards borrowing, that will have to come after powers of taxation have been conferred, but I fear it will be some time before we are actually able to take these steps,"

VII. The Opium Fund.

Our financial position during the three years, 1909-10 to 1911-12 was as follows:—

	Gross Revenue	Gross expenditure	Surplus
	£	£	£
1909-10	74,593,495	73,986,854	606,641
1910-11	80,682,473	76,746,186	3,936,287
1911-12	82,835,750	78,895,416	3,940,334

The revised estimates for 1910-1911 showed surplus of 3½ millions exclusive of grants amounting to a total of 1¾ millions made to Local Governments for various purposes. Thus the true surplus came to £ 5¼ millions or 8 crores. Owing to a defect in the Council rules, nothing could be said or done with respect to the grants made during the current year and criticism was to be confined to what had been proposed in the financial statement. The surplus for 1910-11 was reduced by £ 1¾ millions, the amount of the grants mentioned above, and £ 3½ millions remained for disposal. This amount was taken as being composed of £ 2 millions representing surplus under opium and £1½ millions as the non-opium surplus. The first of these two amounts, it was proposed to devote to the reduction of debt and the second to pass on into the cash balances of the country. Owing to the difficulty referred to above, Mr. Gokhale had to word the Resolution he moved on 7th March 1911 as follows:—"That this Council recommends that the amount of the new loan for next year be raised from £5,925,300 to £7,925,300 and that the extra two millions be set apart to constitute a new fund called the Opium Fund, or in the alternative, be devoted to non-recurring expenditure on Education, Sanitation and Medical Relief." This extra £2 millions would not have increased the indebtedness of the country, because the Government was reducing debt by 2 millions taken out of the opium surplus and in the new year the debt would only have been restored to the original figure. The essence of the proposal was this. Government was calculating upon the total extinction of the opium revenue in 7 years, the annual reduction being 85 lakhs. This steady loss was provided for, no doubt; but if the end came earlier than it was anticipated, Mr. Gokhale said, Government should have a definite resource to draw upon and it could be ensured by the opium surpluses being accumulated in a special fund, particularly as these surpluses were the result of fancy prices paid for the drug by the Chinese people.

The anxiety of Government to reduce our national debt was extraordinary and was justified in the interests of the maintenance of India's credit in the London market. But our unproductive debt was too small to account for this extreme solicitude, and surpluses were being continually devoted to the reduction of debt. Mr. Gokhale was not unconscious of the necessity of a Sinking Fund and was prepared to agree to a definite arrangement being made in that behalf. Compared with the public debts of other nations our burden was nothing. Even in India, he was willing to allow 2 crores annually to get rid of our small debt of 37 crores. That would mean a Sinking Fund of 4 per cent. as against 1 per cent. in England. He observed:—"Surely the Hon'ble Member should be satisfied with this and all money over and above this amount ought to be available for other pressing purposes which require large outlay very badly. Sir, for these purposes—Education, Sanitation and Medical Relief—while a great deal of recurring expenditure is, no doubt, necessary,—there is also a vast amount of non-recurring expenditure absolutely required. And the need is most urgent." He then went on to describe how disappointingly backward our condition was in the matter of primary education and sanitation. This policy he had been advocating, year after year, but without any result. To the Finance Member he was indeed grateful for the way he had provided a million for Education and Sanitation as no predecessor of his had done. "One million is good," said Mr. Gokhale, "but three millions would be better." The Hon'ble Mr. Meston and the Finance Member having opposed the Resolution, it goes without saying, it was rejected.

Lucidity of exposition is a quality which is found to characterise many a financial statement, but in this matter Mr. Gokhale was unequalled. We could give any number of passages from his speeches which are marked with this quality in a pre-eminent degree. We take the liberty of quoting here one rather lengthy passage from his speech he made in support of his Resolution regarding the Opium Fund, and it is Gladstonian in clearness and simplicity. In the following passage Mr. Gokhale showed what was the nature, the composition and the position of the Indian public debt. He said:—

"Sir, what is the amount of our debt? Our total debt is made up of various component factors. There is the permanent or funded debt. There s orary or unfunded debt. And there are various funds with the Government, such as Savings Banks deposits, Service funds, special loans, judicial deposits in courts and so forth. Against this the Government have their Railways and Irrigation works, their loans and advances to Local Bodies, Native States and cultivators, and their cash balances. Deducting these latter from the total debt, what remains is the true ordinary or unproductive debt. Now, taking the figures for 1907—08, and bringing them up to date, we find that in 1907—08 the permanent debt in India was 88. 55 millions; the permanent debt in England was 156·48 millions, or, in the two countries together, 245 millions. That was the funded, permanent debt in that year. The unfunded debt in that year was only 1 million. Then about 20 millions represented special loans, Service funds, Savings Banks deposits, departmedtal and Judicial deposits and miscellaneous obligations of the Government, or total liabilities of 266·28 millions or 400 crores of the liabilities of the Government. As against this, the Government of India had in that year 177·7 millions invested in Railways and 29·87 in Irrigation Works, or a total of 207·57 millions under the two heads together. The Railway debt was earning about 5 per cent., the Irrigat on debt about 7 per cent. Therefore it was really no debt at all in the sense in which the term debt is used. That accounted for 207 out of 266 millions. Then the loans and advances by Government to various Local Bodies, Native States and cultivators amounted in that year to 13 millions and the cash balances were 18·6 millions. Thus, 239 millions out of 267·28 millions represented the investments and cash balances of the Government, leaving only about 27 millions of real unproductive debt for the country. This was in 1907—08. Since then the position has undergone some deterioration. Of course there has been additional borrowing for Railways and Irrigation; but we need not take that into account since Railway and Irrigation investments are earning 5 and 7 per cent. interest respectively But there was a deficit in 1908-09 of 3·74 millions. In 1909-10 there was a surplus of ·61 million, and this year, excluding the opium-surplus of 5 millions, there is still a surplus of ·49 or half a million. The position therefore during the last 3 years ha undergone a deterioration by about 2·64 millions, and we must add thas to the figure for 1907-08 to find the total unproductive debt at the pret sent moment. This comes to 29·7 millions, say 30 millions. Or, if the Finance Minister will prefer it, I am prepared to take the funded unproductive debt, as it appears in our accounts, which is 37 millions. That means making a present of about 7 millions to the Hon'ble Member ; but I will do so and will take 37 millions for the purposes of my argument. Now, Sir, what is a total unproductive debt of 37 millions for a vast country like India? What is such a debt, compared with the huge debts of other countries? And is the reduction of this trifling debt a matter of such paramount importance that everything the Finance Department can lay hands on should be devoted to this reduction to the practical exclusion of all other useful objects, as has been done during the last 10 or 12 years? Sir, my protest against this policy of the Government has been a long-standing one. Year after year, for the last 10 years, I have been raising my voice in this Council against this policy; but so far without much effect. How does our unproductive debt compare with that of other countries? In England, at the present moment, you have a national debt of over 700 millions, correspouding to our unproductive debt. In France it is over a thousand millions. In several other countries it is four to five hundred millions. Even in an Eastern country like China it is about 110 millions, though the annual revenue of China is much smaller than ours. The Hon'ble Member speaks of the necessity of strengthening our credit. If we look at the rates of interest at which different countries borrow, it will be found that our credit is exceedingly good."

VIII. Free Trade and Protection.

In the First Chapter of this book,* we have related the circumstances under which the present cotton excise duties came to be imposed upon the cloth produced in Indian mills, in 1895. They were absolutely indefensible, but sixteen years' continued

---

* See Pages 34-37.

agitation had made little impression upon Government. On 9th March 1911, the Hon'ble Mr. Dadabhoy moved a resolution in the Viceregal Council recommending the abolition of the countervailing duties. He used all the old arguments in favour of their repeal and quoted high authorities to show how the impost had been forced upon an unwilling Government cf India. The continued depression of the Indian industry was also urged as a fresh argument. The Hon'ble Mr. Dadabhoy was supported by almost all Indian members and the case could not have been made stronger. Mr. Gokhale's speech on this occasion was important owing to the pronouncement he made on the question of Indian protectionism. As elsewhere, we have even in this country, our free-trade-protection controversy, and the excise cotton duties have been mainly defended on the ground they are calculated not only to give the Government a much-needed revenue, but to countervail the protection which the import duty of 3½ per cent. gives to the producers of cloth i Indian mills. In the absence of a countervailing duty, it is contended, these millowners would levy a tax upon the consumers and also compete unfairly with handloom weavers. The excise duties undoubtedly fall upon the poorest classes of this country, and it was on their behalf and not that of millowners, that Mr. Gokhale advocated the repeal of that impost. He was not much impressed with the argument about the depressing condition of the indigenous industry which had its ups and downs.

The loss which the abolition would entail, he suggested, might be made good by raising the import duties to 5 per cent., the countervailing duty in India being limited to counts above 30 and being also raised to the corresponding level.

Mr. Gokhale gave expression to his fiscal faith in the following words:—

"In the same way Free Trade for all countries may be all right in theory, but it will be a long, long day before we shall have it in practice everywhere. And till that time comes, every country must take care of its economic interests in its own way. Now, Sir, most countries have adopted protection as their economic policy. It is, however, necessary to remember that there are two kinds of protection, the right kind and the wrong kind. The right kind of protection is that under which the growing industries of a country receive the necessary stimulus and encouragement and support that they require, but under which care is taken that no influential combinations, prejudicial to the interests of the community, come into existence. The wrong kind of protection, on the other hand, is that under which powerful influences and combinations and interests receive assistance to the prejudice of the general community, the general tax-payers of the country. And I believe that the right kind of protection, if available, will do good to India. But, Sir, situated as India is, I fear that there is no likelihood of that kind of protection being available to us, and it is my deliberate conviction that, in our present circumstances, a policy of Free Trade, reasonably applied is, after all, the *safest* policy for us. If the Government of this country were conducted in accordance with the wishes and the opinions of the people, not merely as imagined by the Government of India, but as ascertained by means of a constitutional machinery existing for the purpose, then of course the situation would be a different one."

The evils of protection, as seen in other countries, were present to Mr. Gokhale's mind and they would he intensified in a country like India where the people have no effective voice in the administration and in shaping the policy of government He was afraid that the huge engine of protection, which is a vast power would be employed not in the interests of the people of India but in the interests of other parties that would dominate and exercise pressure on the highest authorities. He concluded:—"That being so, I do not think we should go in for the advocacy of protection, as such, in the present state of the country, and I, for one, will not be a party to such advocacy. I do not therefore join in the plea that the abolition of excise duties would be a measure of protection to the Indian industry and that the Government should acceede to it on that ground. But independently of that we have a strong case for urging that these duties should be abolished." Mr. Gokhale felt that in this matter of securing the right kind of protection, there was really not much to choose between the two parties in England. We would draw the earnest attention of the reader to these passages we have quoted from Mr. Gokhale's speech and ask him to ponder over the sound principle enunciated with regard to fiscal policy in India. There is so much loose talk on this subject, that careful thought has to be bestowed upon every scheme of protection or inter-imperial free trade that may be proposed for our adoption.

Another opportunity presented itself to Mr. Gokhale the same day to develop his ideas on the subject of protection, and was provided by the Hon'ble Pandit Madan Mohan Malaviya's Resolution in the Viceroy's Council, which recommended that the duty on imported sugar be so raised as to make it possible for the indigenous sugar industry to survive the competition to which it was exposed. The mover of the Resolution reviewed the history of the Indian sugar industry and showed how it had recently fallen upon very bad times in spite of the many advantages this country enjoyed with respect to its development. He put in a strong plea for protection and said that personally he was not afraid to suggest a duty of even 30 per cent. or more if necessary for the conservation of that ancient industry of India. Mr. Gokhale moved an amendment to the Resolution of Pandit Madan Mohan and the latter accepted it. It was as follows:—"That this Council recommends that the Government should order an inquiry by a Committee of competent persons into the present condition of the sugar industry in India with a view to ascertaining what action can and should be taken by the State to save the industry from the threatened ruin." It was quite clear from the smallest calculation that if the indigenous industry was to be protected against foreign competition, a duty of from 40 to 100 per cent. would have to be imposed upon the imports according to the kind of sugar that was to be protected. Following the line of reasoning he had taken up earlier the same day, Mr. Gokhale pointed out how industries in a backward country like India required protection at the hands of the State when they were confronted with competition from well-organized and large-scale foreign manufactures. But in the peculiar political circumstances of this country, he thought, the kind of protection resorted to in other nations was impossible. He therefore thought that 'for the present he should ask the State to give only such help to the industry as it can, without running counter to the principles which are at present in the ascendant in the administration of this country ' viz. free trade principles. Various questions were obviouly involved in the discussion of Mr. Malaviya's Resolution. On whom would the proposed duty fall ? Who would gain or suffer directly from the protective duty ? What would be the position of the cultivators and the general mass of taxpayers ? And Mr. Gokhale thought that most 'of the Indian sugar factories being in European hands, a 30 per cent duty on sugar would only take 2 crores out of the pockets of a poor class whose earnings were between Rs. 100 and Rs. 1,000 a year, and transfer the sum practically to the pockets of English manufacturers of sugar in the country. Under the circumstances, the whole problem required careful inquiry and consideration and if protective measures were to be taken, as certainly they must be taken, each case must be judged on its own merits.

IX. Regime of Lord Hardinge.

Several Resolutions on administrative and other reforms were moved by Mr. Gokhale in the course of the two years 1911 and 1912. He had taken up the question of free and compulsory elementary education and fought hard for it in the Viceregal Council. Employment of Indians in the Public Service, Police reform, advisory district boards, the resources of local bodies and such other topics also were handled by him with the wonderful ability so characterastic of him, and the South African question and abolition of indentured labour generally, found in him one of the most active and effective agitators. These years likewise witnessed important events,the most significant of which were the visit of their Most Gracious Imperial Majesties, the King-Emperor and Queen Empress of India, the magnificient Delhi Durbar, the annulment of the partition of Bengal and the elevation of that Province to the status of a Presidency ruled by a Governor-in-Council and the transfer of the cipital of India from Calcutta to Delhi. These were momentous changes :and made a profound impression upon the country. The year 1911--12 Lord Hardinge very happily characterised as an *annus mirabilis* and as one calculated, owing to the beneficent administrative changes announced by the King-Emperor at Delhi, to leave a lasting mark upon the history of India. Reviewing the general situation His Excellency the Viceroy said:—" The situation has now entirely changed ; the dark shadows that lay over us have passed away. Our taxation has been lightened. The resources of Local Governments have been strengthened. Exchange is stable and however much opinions may differ on points of detail, I believe that the basis of our currency policy is secured in public confidence. So also with our military dispositions. The momentous change that the Russian Agreement brought into our relations with our great Asiatic neighbour removed the menace on our frontier and the rapid growth of our army expenditure has now been checked and curtailed. At first these improvements were obcured by the financial collapse of 1907 and our slow recovery from its effects. But with care and economy our finances are restored to health ; the sky is clear so far as human eye can judge and we are ready for our next advance." The key-note of the advance was to be the spread of knowledge and a resolute struggle against avoidable disease. The noble-mindedness of the Viceroy, his far-sighted statesmanship and his courage in standing up for the interests and dignity of India, endeared Lord Hardinge to the heart of the people, who felt that no such Viceroy had been sent out to this country since the time of Lord Ripon. At a very difficult conjuncture in India's history, he held the helm of Government with a courage, an unerring judgment and a true appreciation of the future of India, so rare among the rulers of the land, and that is why his administration became a land-mark in the histroy of this country.

That the Council reforms of 1909 had proved a success, every one frankly acknowledged. As to the services rendered by the Supreme Legislative Council, Sir Guy said:—"But I can testify unhesitatingly to the power the Council holds for good in directing attention to the finances of the country, in scrutinizing expenditure and in advising the Government on the employment of the public funds. I have always found the criticisms of my non-official colleagues temperate, suggestive and helpful. . . It is no exaggeration to say that the free interchange of views which this Council stimulates, has already become a powerful factor for good in the financial policy of India." In his budget speech of 1912, Mr. Gokhale again took a masterly review of the financial situation and thought that in view of the many difficult aspects of it which arrested attention at the time, an inquiry by a Royal Commission had become necessary. He noted three outstanding features of the position:—"A top-heavy administration, much too costly for our resources, a crushing weight of military burdens, and a scheme of taxation which, though not much more burdensome in its total incidence than in other countries, presses much more heavily on the poorer than on the middle and the upper classes of the community."

X. Gokhale and Gladstone.

The beginning of the end of Mr. Gokhale's public career and life had come and it was visible to everyone who had anything to do with him. He was overworking himself and knew neither rest nor respite from his intense and incessant toil. He had set his heart upon the big reform in the matter of compulsory education, the South African question required his constant attention and the work of the Public Services Commission was one which absorbed a good deal of his energy. Like the late Mr. Justice Ranade, Mr. Gokhale cared not for his health or comfort or convenience before the cause of his country's well-being. To work and toil, night and day, had become a second nature with him. His friends felt deep anxiety for his health, but no one could venture to advise him to cease work and those who did, had absolutely no hopes of succeeding. He thus wore himself out like his *guru* and had the satisfaction of laying himself on the altar of his country's good. Summing up the budget debate on 25th March, 1912, Sir Guy Fleetwood Wilson made the following observations in this connection:—"The Hon'ble Mr. Gokhale reminds me of Mr. Gladstone. On one occasion, when Mr. Gladstone was suffering from the effects of ovrwork, he was ordered by his physician complete rest. By way of carrying out the orders of his physician, he promptly bought a Turkish Grammar and proceeded to study that language." This was exactly a peculiar characteristic of Mr. Ranade. He was never more uncomfortable than when he had no work to do. Towards the close of his life, he was in indifferent health and was contemplating the taking of leave if not of retiring. Doctors had frequently advised rest. But that was absolutely impossible. Work seemed more necessary to his life, pradoxial as it may appear, than food or rest. Sir Guy proceeded to observe:—"Mr. Gokhale, to the intense regret of every one in this room, is admittedly suffering from the effects of overwork. I have little doubt that his medical adviser has enjoined him to avoid all unnecessary effort. By way of carrying out those instructions, he takes advantage of fifteen brief minutes at his disposal to embark on a discussion on such a trifle as a review of the whole basis of taxation."

On 27th February 1912, the Hon'ble Mr. Dadabhoy moved a Resolution recommending that the minimum of income assessable to the Income-tax be raised, from Rs. 1,000, the existing limit, to Rs. 1,500 a year. The proposal did not meet with Mr. Gokhale's approval. He had, no doubt, striven all along for the reduction of the burden of taxation on the shoulders of the people, but Mr. Dadabhoy's suggestion sought to grant relief to a class of tax-payers which was not entitled to that concession in view of the burden of the lower classes and the financial situation in the country. There were numerous calls of an urgent nature upon the national purse, and it could not afford to lose the contribution made by the income-tax-paying class of the community. Mr. Gokhale contended:—"The State has to look at the whole scheme of taxation-first, from the stand-point of its own necessities, and, secondly, from the stand point of the comparative ability of the different classes to pay their particular share of the total revenue raised from the community. Now, judged by this standard, I really do not think that the class for which my Hon'ble friend seeks a remission has any substantial grievance." It is an accepted fact that the poorer classes in India bear a larger burden than the upper and middle classes, and though high prices were calculated to cause some hardship to the latter, the national scheme of taxation must always be considered as a whole and not from the point of view of this class or the other. Mr Gokhale agreed with the mover of the Resolution that the principle of abatement should be introduced into this country and that while the minimum taxable limit should be kept at Rs. 1,000, there should be some abatement granted to those, who were just above that limit. He also agreed that in the case of joint stock companies or those who had an income of Rs. 50,000 a year there might be a little higher rate of taxation.

XI. Last Efforts.

Mr. Gokhale made his last budget speech in the Viceregal Council in 1912. To the last, he was anxious to take his usual part in the deliberations of that legislative body, but serious illness prevented him from doing so. But during that year he moved a number of resolutions on important subjects and thus made full use of the opportunities provided to non-officials members by the Council reforms, to agitate for measures of public utility. Thus in March, 1912, he urged that the amount of the loan to be raised during the next year be increased by one crore of rupees, so that the expenditure proposed to be incurred for building new Delhi in 1912-13 should be met entirely out of loan funds and not partly out of next year's estimated surplus.

The resolution involved the old principle about the use of surpluses and the reduction of debt. Of the three courses open to the Government to meet the charges of new Delhi, the Finance Member preferred that of putting the Delhi works on precisely the same footing as our large railway and irrigation works, treating them as capital expenditure and financing them partly from loans and partly from whatever spare revenues remained in each year after meeting the ordinary administrative needs. It meant that surpluses, which represent excess of revenue over the amount needed for the ordinary expenditure, taken out of the packets of the people, were going to be devoted indirectly to the reduction of the unproductive debt and not to measures calculated to promote the well-being of the people. With regard to this point Mr. Gokhale said:—"This, however, has been one of the principal grievances which non-official members have urged in this Council again and again for several years past. I, for one, have been raising my humble voice year after year, against the misapplication of our surpluses since I entered this Council now eleven years ago. Year after year, I have been pointing out that while this may be sound Finance in the West, it is not sound finance in this country, where the unproductive debt is really a very small amount." Mr. Gokhale contrasted the conditions in other countries with the peculiar circumstances of India and contended that 'in this country a surplus is always a temptation to the Government either to pay off its debt faster than is necessary, or else increase expenditure in directions which entirely depend upon its own will and which sometimes do not commend themselves to the people.

In moving another Resolution on the same day recommending the creation of special Provincial Reserves by means of grants from Imperial surpluses, Mr. Gokhale drove home the same contention and crystalised it in two definite points: (1) taking the smallness of our unproductive debt into consideration, there is no need to liquidate it out of our ordinary surpluses—the provision that already exists for redemption of capital under railways for reduction or avoidance of debt under famine insurance, being amply sufficient for the purpose; and (2) but money is required for non-recurring expenditure in many directions in this country, especially for education, sanitation and medical relief. His idea, therefore, was that having made reasonable provision for the liquidation of debt annually, if that is absolutely necessary, the remaining portion of the surpluses should be made over to the Provincial Governments to form the nucleus of Provincial reserves for non-recurring expenditure on education, sanitation and medical relief. He wanted to fix a certain proportion of the surpluses viz. two-thirds, for being handed over to Local Governments. That would be an obligation thrown upon the Government af India, as the Local Governments would be obliged to spend the sums thus received on programmes of non-recurring expenditure mentioned above.

One of the many objects Mr. Gokhale had at heart relating to the well-being of the masses, was the strengthening of the resources of Local Bodies in the different Provinces so as to enable them to discharge the duties entrusted to them, in an efficient manner. He therefore moved a Resolution recommending the appointment of a committee of officials and non-officials to inquire into the adequacy or otherwise of the resources of these bodies. The Decentralizatiou Commission had gone into this question and there was hardly any difference of opinion as to the need of good water supply, sanitation, primary education and so forth in our villages and as to the most inadequate resources that were at the disposal of the Local Bodies. Mr. Gokhale was able to make out a strong case easily, and though Government did not concede his demand for a committee of inquiry, they gave an assurance that the views expressed in the course of the discussion would receive consideration when the question would be disposed of. He had never the delusion that his resolutions would be accepted by Government in the Council and that the policy he advocated would be received with frank approval. Yet he raised debates on matters in which he wanted reforms to be introduced and brought home to the mind of Government and the country the reasonableness and urgency of his proposals. This advocacy told upon Government all the same, and

Mr. Gokhale's suggestions were quietly adopted in the measures taken in subsequent years.*

In a resolution he moved in the Viceroy's Council in March 1912, the Hon'ble Sir Vithaldas Thackersay raised the question of the throwing open of Indian mints to the free coinage of gold. This question was subsequently discussed by the Chamberlain Commission on Indian Finance and Currency, which did not feel that a gold currency was at all needed for India. The matter has been long under discussion between the Government of India, the Secretary of State and the British Treasury. The Government of India in their latest despatch on the question, warmly supported the coinage of sovereigns or a ten rupee gold coin in the Indian mints, but the proposal was not favourably received by the Treasury and the question awaited the recommendation of the Chamberlain Commission. From what we have said in a previous chapter about the relation between high prices and currency and Mr. Gokhale's views on that question, it will be apparent that he was in favour of a gold currency being introduced into this country and gold pieces being coined in the Indian mints. We know Mr. Gokhale was asked and intended to submit his views on the whole currency problem to the Chamberlain Commission and he told the writer of this volume that he could not do so for want of time. But we know what he would have said. In supporting Sir Vithaldas Thackersay's resolution he

* See pages 3-4.

once more demonstrated how the Quantitative Theory of money applied to cases of backword countries like India and elaborated his views in that behalf again. He wanted an automatic and self-adjusting currency in India and spoke as follows:—

"The Fowler Committee and other authorities have advocated a gold standard and a gold currency not a silver currency, as the permanent arrangement for this country. The time has come when we should consider whether we should not enter on the next stage of our currency policy and go in for the coinage of gold pieces, admitting silver, however, for the present, to unlimited legal tender. But a time must come when silver will have to be restricted in amount as legal tender, and gold will then have to be the principal coin of the country."

INDEX